CALORIE
COUNTER

ROBIN HINDSON
HARGITA STAFFORD

PENGUIN BOOKS

Penguin Books Australia Ltd
487 Maroondah Highway, PO Box 257
Ringwood, Victoria 3134, Australia
Penguin Books Ltd
Harmondsworth, Middlesex, England
Viking Penguin, A Division of Penguin Books USA Inc.
375 Hudson Street, New York, New York 10014, USA
Penguin Books Canada Limited
10 Alcorn Avenue, Toronto, Ontario, Canada M4V 3B2
Penguin Books (N.Z.) Ltd
182–190 Wairau Road, Auckland 10, New Zealand

First published by Penguin Books Australia Ltd 1992
2nd edition 1994
3rd edition 1994

10 9 8 7 6 5 4 3 2 1

Typeset in Helvetica Medium/Light Condensed
by Bookset, Melbourne
Printed in Australia by Australian Print Group, Maryborough

National Library of Australia
Cataloguing-in-Publication data

Hindson, Robin.
The Australian calorie counter.

3rd ed.
ISBN 0 14 024142 6.

1. Food – Calorie content – Tables. 2. Food – Sodium content
– Tables. 3. Food – Cholesterol content – Tables. I. Stafford, Hargita H. II. Title.

641. 1042

CONTENTS

Authors
Robin Hindson DIMgt CertDiet DipEd RD
Lecturer in Nutrition and Food Service, School of Nutrition and Public Health, Deakin University

Dr Hargita Stafford BSc(Nutr), Grad.Dip.Diet., PhD(Nutr)
Researcher in Public Health Nutrition, Food and Nutrition Program, School of Nutrition and Public Health, Deakin University

Editorial and research
Jane Angus, Jenny Lang, Barbara Weiss, Frances Waterman, Catherine Cooper, Sandra Ellemor

Acknowledgements
The authors and publishers would like to thank the many food manufacturers for contributing and approving the nutritional information regarding their products.

Data for the nutrient composition of Australian meats, fruits and vegetables are copyright to Associate Professor Heather Greenfield, and other authors, at the Department of Food Science and Technology, University of New South Wales, and are reproduced and used with permission.

The following sources are gratefully acknowledged.

Composition of Foods Australia, AGPS, Canberra, 1989.

Dietary Allowances for Use in Australia, National Health and Medical Research Council, AGPS, Canberra, 1989.

Food Australia (formerly *Food Technology in Australia*), journal of the Council of Australian Food Technology Associations and the Australian Institute of Food Science and Technology, nos 1–45, 1979–89.

Food for Health, R. English and J. Lewis, National Food Authority, Canberra, 1992.

HOW TO USE THIS BOOK

There are seven sections.

1 **How to use this book** explains how foods are listed and described, and how quantities are judged.
2 **Health and eating habits** describes the components of a healthy diet; shows how to determine your healthy weight range; explains the recommendations of the Dietary Guidelines for Australians; and gives detailed advice about weight control, including charts and exercise plans.
3 The **Alcohol** section gives you information about the effects of alcohol on health; discusses safe intake levels; includes hints for regulating your consumption; and lists the alcoholic content of standard drinks.
4 The **Counter** is a detailed alphabetical list that provides you with kilojoule and calorie (food-energy) values for handy quantities of a huge range of foods (including brands) and drinks (including alcoholic drinks).
5 The **Introduction to the Table** provides health information about fat, cholesterol, sodium (and salt), calcium and dietary fibre, and explains how to include the right amount of each in your diet.
6 The **Table** is an alphabetical list giving the fat, cholesterol, sodium, calcium and dietary fibre content for a wide range of foods (including brands) arranged in selected food groups.
7 The **Vitamin Guide** explains what vitamins are, why you need them, how deficiencies occur and how best to make sure that your vitamin intake is adequate. It also includes specific information and tables for thirteen important vitamins.

USING THE COUNTER AND THE TABLE

In these two sections foods and drinks are listed alphabetically (use the easy-find page headings). Under the main items, types are listed first by description and then by brand name; for example under *anchovies*, 'canned' and 'raw' are followed by 'Admiral' and 'John West'.

In the Counter, large listings (for example, *biscuits*) are in italic type to help you further. In the Table, *all* foods are grouped in large listings, for example *'Take-away and Convenience Meals'*. Where foods come under the same category and have the same energy value, they appear together, separated by a slash (/). For example, under *beans, mixed*, two brand names are given thus: 'Masterfoods/ Edgell'.

QUANTITIES AND VALUES

In some cases figures have been rounded off: this is because serving sizes vary (for example the weight of a 'medium-sized' apple may vary with one's estimation of 'medium'); and because there are variations according to season, degree of freshness, recipe and pre-paration (for example how much fat is trimmed from meat). Within these limits, however, the figures are reliable and may be used confidently to calculate the approximate energy value of your food (in kilojoules or calories) as well as the fat, cholesterol, sodium, calcium and dietary fibre values.

Figures in the **Sample food and exercise diary** (pp. 19–20) are broadly representative: use the Counter to establish quantities and values for your own food diary.

DESCRIPTIONS OF FOODS

If no specific description is given the figures apply to the part of the food normally eaten, for example *beans, broad* will include the bean seeds but not the pods.

Where it is appropriate there is a description to help you estimate quantities in a practical way; for example the figure for *pasta ... dried* should be used if you measure before cooking, and *pasta ... boiled* if you estimate a serving size on your plate.

Unless specifically requested by the company concerned, all product names in the Counter are given in lower-case letters.

HEALTH AND EATING HABITS

~~~~~~

CHOOSING HEALTHY EATING

Not only is our food varied and excellent in quality; it is also available in great quantity. If, however, we combine a sedentary lifestyle with eating more than we need, we become prone to the 'Western diseases of affluence' – obesity, high blood pressure, stroke, heart disease, diabetes, gall-bladder disease and cancer.

Fortunately, good nutrition and good health can go hand in hand. We can exercise choice about what we eat.

If you want to eat for health you should know about the **Dietary Guidelines for Australians** issued by the Commonwealth Department of Health in 1992. There are ten broad guidelines. (For details see 'A closer look at the Dietary Guidelines', p. 10.)

1   Enjoy a wide variety of nutritious foods.
2   Eat plenty of breads and cereals (preferably wholegrain), vegetables (including legumes) and fruits.
3   Eat a diet low in fat and, in particular, low in saturated fat.
4   Maintain a healthy body weight by balancing physical activity and food intake.
5   If you drink alcohol, limit your intake.
6   Eat only a moderate amount of sugars and foods containing added sugars.
7   Choose low-salt foods and use salt sparingly.
8   Encourage and support breastfeeding.
9   Eat foods containing calcium. This is particularly important for girls and women.

10 Eat foods containing iron. This applies particularly to girls, women, vegetarians and athletes.

UNDERSTANDING YOUR WEIGHT

For weight control, follow guidelines 1–6, but first check your desirable weight range from the **height–weight chart**.

Height–weight chart: aged 18 onwards

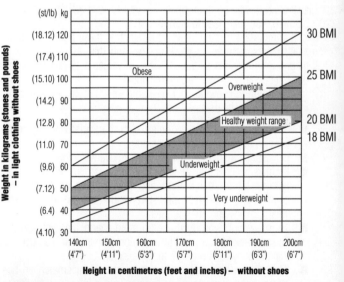

Based on the recommendations of the National Health and Medical Research Council (October 1984). Adapted from the Australian Nutrition Foundation Chart.

Your body type, including your bone structure, is genetically determined, and will be one factor in determining your weight. For this reason, and because height influences weight, your desirable weight will fall within a range rather than being fixed.

You can also understand more about your weight by working out your **Body Mass Index** (BMI), using the following formula.

$$BMI = \frac{\text{weight in kilograms}}{\text{height in metres x height in metres}}$$

For most people a normal BMI is between 20 and 25; if your BMI is above 25 it *may* be appropriate for you to lose weight, and if it's below 20 you *may* need to gain weight.

It's important to remember, however, that these figures relate to healthy persons over 18 years of age, and that, as in the case of height–weight charts or tables, they are valuable as references but don't necessarily apply to every individual.

In addition to knowing your desirable weight range, the following information may be useful.

■ The importance given to being slim, particularly in regard to women, is partly a matter of fashion.
■ In Australia more men than women are overweight.
■ From a health point of view it is less harmful to be a 'pear' (excess fat on the bottom and thighs) than an 'apple' (fat overhanging the waistline). Overweight women tend to be 'pears', overweight men 'apples'.
■ To lose weight you must use up more energy than you take in. To gain weight you must take in more energy than you use, so that the body can convert it to new tissue.
■ 'Going on a diet' and crash dieting are not recommended because, apart from possibly missing some important nutrients, the result may be a slowing-down of your metabolic rate, so that

your body uses less energy; then when you eat normally again you may put weight back on because your body is not using all the energy available. It is better to make a permanent change to nutritional eating habits and a healthy lifestyle. Mild food-energy restriction (up to 2100 kJ/500 Cal per day) does not seem to trigger a slowing-down of metabolism.

■ Rapid weight loss may involve losing fluid, lean-muscle tissue and important stores of energy, leading to fatigue and head-aches. It is better to reduce weight slowly and to lose fat only.

It followed me home!

CALCULATING YOUR ENERGY INTAKE

Food energy is measured in **kilojoules** (kJ) or **kilocalories** (kcal or Cal). 'Kilocalories' may be abbreviated to 'calories' in common usage. In this book both measurements are given. One Cal (1 kcal) = 4.184 (approximately 4.2) kJ.

A convenient way to calculate the food energy for a healthy weight-loss diet is to allow a set amount per day, for example 5000–7500 kilojoules (1200–1800 calories), depending on age and activity level. Nutritious foods should then be selected to meet these energy levels (see 'Losing weight with a food diary', p.16).

The following table sets out the energy used in various levels of activity.

Energy expenditure for a range of activities

Energy expenditure (kJ/Cal)	Occupational	Recreational
Very light activity (less than 10 kJ/ 2 Cal per minute)	standing, with light activity (e.g. sales assistant) typing (electrical)	eating sleeping driving a car strolling sewing knitting
Light activity (10–20 kJ/ 2–5 Cal per minute)	farm work (mechanised) assembly work light industry typing (manual) housework bricklaying driving a truck	light gardening gymnastics billiards fishing bowling slow walking (4 km/h)
Moderate activity (20–30 kJ/ 5–7 Cal per minute)	general labouring (pick and shovel) painting farm work (non-mechanised)	heavy gardening golf (carrying clubs) tennis (doubles) cycling (16 km/h) cricket table tennis moderate walking (5.5 km/h)
Heavy activity (30–40 kJ/ 7–10 Cal per minute)	coalmining heavy labouring	skipping jogging football tennis (singles) skiing (vigorous downhill) climbing stairs basketball moderate swimming
Very heavy activity (more than 40kJ/ 10 Cal per minute)	lumber work (non mechanised)	squash running cross-country skiing cycling (racing) fast swimming

Table courtesy of the National Heart Foundation

KEEPING UP THE NUTRIENTS

When you reduce your intake of kilojoules you may also reduce your intake of other important nutrients – protein, carbohydrate, dietary fibre, vitamins and minerals. The way to maintain your intake of these nutrients is to eat less of the most concentrated energy sources (for example fat and alcohol) and sufficient of the least concentrated (protein and carbohydrate). The following table sets out the energy values for these four sources.

Energy value of energy-containing nutrients

NUTRIENT	ENERGY	
	kJ/g	Cal/g
Protein	17	4
Carbohydrate	17	4
Fat	37	9
Alcohol	29	7

From this table it can be seen that foods high in **fat** are concentrated sources of energy. These foods include butter, margarine, vegetable oils, fried foods, cream, chocolate, and many cakes, biscuits, pastries, cheeses and types of ice-cream. You need some fat in your diet to supply essential fatty acids and fat-soluble vitamins, but your total intake should be kept low (see also 'A closer look at the Dietary Guidelines', p. 10, and 'Fat', p. 169).

Alcohol, another concentrated energy source, is not an essential nutrient. (See also 'A closer look at the Dietary Guidelines' below, and 'Alcohol', p. 29).

Protein foods supply relatively smaller amounts of energy unless they are accompanied by fat; for example lean meat is low in energy but fatty meat is high, and low-fat and skim milks are lower in energy value than whole milk.

Carbohydrate foods such as rice, pasta, sugar-free wholegrain breakfast cereals, bread, potatoes and other fruits and vegetables are lower in energy and so can be eaten more freely. At least 50 per cent of daily energy should come from carbohydrate foods; but remember not to add fatty toppers, sauces or spreads.

A CLOSER LOOK AT THE DIETARY GUIDELINES

The Dietary Guidelines for Australians includes the following specific information about diet.

Guideline 1 involves eating foods daily from each of the five main food groups.

1   Milk and milk products.
2   Meat, poultry, fish, and meat alternatives such as peas, beans, lentils, eggs and nuts.
3   Vegetables and fruit.
4   Bread and cereals.
5   Butter or table margarine (one tablespoon daily).

A balanced diet of about 5000 kilojoules (1200 calories) per day can be made up of:

■ low-fat milk (300 ml), yoghurt (300 ml) or cheese (40 g)
■ one to two serves of lean meat or meat alternative. (One serve equals 100 grams meat or poultry, 150 grams fish, two eggs, 20 grams nuts, or 3⁄4 cup legumes)
■ five different vegetables cooked or as salad, and two pieces of whole fresh fruit (cooked or canned fruit or fruit juice without sugar may be substituted for one serve)
■ six slices of wholemeal bread, or six serves of either wholegrain cereals, brown rice or pasta
■ water to drink. Water contains no kilojoules; use it to quench thirst instead of sweetened soft drinks, fruit juices, alcoholic drinks or high-fat, flavoured milk and milk-substitute drinks.

See also **Sample food and exercise diary**, p. 19, for information about recommended servings for a slightly higher daily food-energy intake.

Guideline 2. These foods supply important vitamins and minerals, including Vitamin C and Vitamin B complex. The foods in this group also supply different types of dietary fibre, each of which has a different function, including reducing levels of blood cholesterol; improving bowel regularity; and giving a feeling of fullness after eating, so helping to avoid over-eating. Because high-fat, high-sugar foods supply such concentrated energy you eat much more of them before you feel full. The opposite is true of high-fibre foods, which make you feel full sooner while supplying less energy: it takes over 500 grams of apples (a high-fibre food) to provide the same energy as 50 grams of chocolate (a high-fat, high-sugar food).

Guideline 3. Fat is the most concentrated source of energy. Compare the energy values for 100 grams each of butter, oil, chips, chocolate and peanut butter with the energy values for

100 grams each of bread, apples and lean chicken fillets: now you know why foods containing fat are the most significant when counting kilojoules! A diet high in saturated fat increases the risk of heart disease.

Guideline 5. Alcohol is a wasteful way of consuming energy because it supplies nothing else that the body needs physiologically. If you enjoy having a drink, limit the number of drinks and try low-alcohol and non-alcohol alternatives. (See 'Alcohol', p. 29).

Guideline 6. In moderation sugar doesn't supply too many kilojoules because it is a pure carbohydrate food; however, it is an extravagant way to consume energy as it provides no other nutrients. If you are trying to lose weight, count out sugar and foods and drinks high in sugar, especially if they are also high in fat – for example cakes, biscuits and confectionery.

Guideline 7. Two elements, sodium and chlorine, make up salt (sodium chloride). Our bodies need some sodium, but from salt added to food many people get too much. A high sodium intake is linked to high blood pressure, which can lead to other health problems. Don't eat too much processed, convenience or take-away food: these foods often have high levels of salt, and are often high in fat and calories as well.

Guideline 10. Deficiency of iron, which can lead to anaemia, is a common problem, particularly in women. Lean red meat is the most useful source of iron. Vitamin C (in fruits and vegetables) aids the absorption of iron, and even small amounts of meat, poultry and fish can make the iron in wholemeal bread, cereals, vegetables, legumes and nuts more available to the body.

The **Healthy diet pyramid** illustrates the recommendations of the Dietary Guidelines.

The Healthy diet pyramid

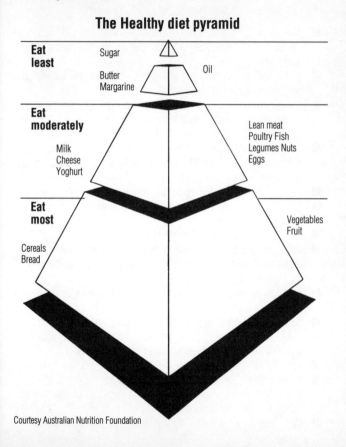

Courtesy Australian Nutrition Foundation

GOLDEN RULES FOR WEIGHT CONTROL

Here are some more strategies to help you lose weight.

- Alter your long-term eating patterns – don't eat 'diet' foods or 'go on a diet', especially a crash diet or one that recommends a 'magic' food.
- Make one or two changes at a time, until you are comfortable with them. Then work on several more.
- Focus on moderation, not deprivation. The occasional indulgence is quite acceptable and won't cause you to revert to unhealthy eating patterns or to binge.
- Remember you are changing eating habits developed over many years. Set a realistic weight goal with intermediate goals, and weigh weekly, not daily.
- Use the Dietary Guidelines for the whole family.
- Eat only at the table – not on the move, when reading, or when watching television.
- Use a smaller plate to serve smaller meals.
- Take just one or two mouthfuls of the food you desire so much, close your eyes and enjoy it. Remind yourself that the rest of the food will taste the same, so you don't need it.
- Eat more slowly. Chew food well, and put down your knife and fork between mouthfuls.
- Keep busy, preferably away from the kitchen and food shops.
- Avoid food-shopping when you're hungry, keep to a shopping list, and don't buy high-energy snacks and nibbles.
- Eat only when you're hungry.
- Keep a supply of low-energy instant snacks – carrot and celery sticks, fruit, orange-juice iceblocks or frozen fruit pieces (orange, watermelon or banana).
- Don't keep food hoards at work, in your handbag, or in the car.

- Avoid fried take-away foods – choose salad rolls, hamburgers with salad, or steak sandwich with salad.
- Look for recipe books that emphasise interesting healthy food.
- Go to the phone instead of the fridge if you're miserable.
- If you are bingeing or have a craving, find out whether you are hungry or just tense, bored, or depressed (bingeing has little to do with hunger). If you're not hungry try exercising or relaxing with an activity you enjoy.
- Use anxiety positively, to find solutions to problems to do something you have been putting off. Turn your desire to eat into a more positive use of your time and energy.
- Nurture yourself with loving attention. Knowing how to care for yourself when you are anxious or run down is a key to your emotional well-being and to long-term weight control.
- Don't punish yourself if you overeat on occasions. Just start again. Think positively and reward yourself for your successes. It's the long term that counts.

You should also be aware of the following:

- It's important to consult a doctor before reducing your energy intake to less than 4200 kilojoules (1000 calories) per day.
- Low-carbohydrate diets are not recommended – a 5000 kJ (1200 calorie) diet should supply at least 150 grams of carbohydrate.
- Many fad diets are dangerous to health, especially if followed long-term.
- Grapefruit is a low-energy fruit but otherwise has no special properties to help you lose weight.
- You can't rub or massage fat away.
- Lean muscle tissue uses more energy than fat tissue.

LOSING WEIGHT WITH A FOOD DIARY

To lose weight, most people will have to cut back their average daily food energy intake by about 2100 kilojoules (500 calories). This is a deficit of 14,600 kilojoules (3500 calories) each week and should promote a weight loss of 0.5 – 1.0 kilograms per week. If you add some daily exercise (see p. 26) the result will be even better, as you will not only burn up kilojoules but stimulate your body to become more efficient at the burning-up process.

Keeping a food diary is helpful for several reasons.

- It makes you more aware of **what** and **when** you eat through the day. The volume and type of food you eat may surprise you.
- It helps you identify faulty eating habits and the triggers (other than hunger) to eating.
- It helps you discover whether you are getting the necessary variety in your diet.
- By charting your progress, it helps motivate you.
- Most important of all, it allows you to start designing your own eating plan.

A tailor-made eating plan is the best and only long-term solution to losing weight and keeping it off. The plan should be flexible and, with modifications (for example reducing your main sources of fat, sugar and alcohol), similar to what you already eat – otherwise you won't stick to it. This approach means you don't have to follow a rigid or complicated diet designed by someone else.

If you have special dietary needs seek advice from a registered dietitian.

How it works

1 Organise a set of charts like the one on p. 18. Photocopy (and perhaps enlarge) this chart, or use a notebook. You may need more or less space for some meals (see also **Sample food and exercise diary**, pp. 19–20). Have one chart for every day of the week for as many weeks as you need to record your intake.

2 Record all that you eat and drink for seven days, but do not cut back on what you would normally eat. Work out the energy value (either in kilojoules or calories) of what you eat every day and add the amounts together to get a total for the week. Divide this by 7 to get your **average daily food energy intake.** If your weight hasn't changed, this is about the energy intake you need to keep your current weight, at your present level of activity. Usually it's 6300– 14,600 kilojoules (1500–3500 calories).

3 Cut your average daily energy intake by about 2100 kilojoules (500 calories). If your average intake is 8400 kilojoules (2000 calories), to lose weight your intake should be around 6300 kilojoules (1500 calories) per day. Go back over your food diary and see where changes can be made so that your intake is reduced by 2100 kilojoules (500 calories) *every day*.

4 Success depends on how you arrive at your new intake. In general, cut back fat (see pp. 171–2). Adapt recipes to make them lower in kilojoules or calories (many can have cream replaced with evaporated skim milk, and much less sugar, butter, margarine and oil).

5 In addition to recording your food and kilojoule or calorie intake, consider whether you are getting the right balance of food and the necessary variety. Make sure your diet includes foods from the basic five food groups (p. 10). This will give you the recommended range of nutrients to keep your body healthy while you are losing weight.

Your food diary

Day Date Food Item	Portion (g or ml)	Food variety								Food (kJ/Cal)	Exercise (kJ/Cal)	Triggers to eating
		Vegetables, legumes	Fruit	Bread, cereals	Milk, dairy	Meat, fish, eggs, nuts	Fats	Other				
Breakfast												
Skim milk in drinks (whole day)												
Snack												
Lunch												
Snack												
Dinner												
Snack												
TOTAL												

A sample food and exercise diary is shown on pp. 19–20 (portion sizes and energy values are generally representative; use the figures in the Counter for your own food diary).

Sample food and exercise diary – 6250kJ (1500 Cal)

| Day Mon. Date 15 Jan. Food item | Portion (g or ml) | Food variety* | | | | | | | Food (kJ/ Cal) | Exercise (kJ/ Cal) | Triggers to eating |
		Vegetables, legumes	Fruit	Bread, cereals	Milk, dairy	Meat, fish, eggs, nuts	Fats	Other			
Breakfast											
1 slice w/meal toast	33	-	-	✔	-	-	-	-	300/70		
butter	5	-	-	-	-	-	✔	-	150/36		hunger
1 tsp vegemite	5	-	-	-	-	-	-	✔	30/7		
wheat flakes	30	-	-	✔	-	-	-	-	430/103		
skim milk	200	-	-	-	✔	-	-	-	290/70		
small banana	70	-	✔	-	-	-	-	-	250/60		
Skim milk in drinks.											
(whole day)	200	-	-	-	✔	-	-	-	290/70		
Snack											anxiety : work pressures
almonds	10	-	-	-	-	✔	-	-	250/60		
raisins	15	-	✔	-	-	-	-	-	170/40		
chocolate	8	-	-	-	-	-	-	✔	209/50		
Lunch										brisk walk after lunch (30 min.) 840/ 200	
2 slices w/meal bread	70	-	-	✔✔	-	-	-	-	310/75		
½ cup tuna in brine	90	-	-	-	-	✔	-	-	490/120		
avocado (as spread)	20	-	✔	-	-	-	-	-	220/50		
3 leaves lettuce	100	✔	-	-	-	-	-	-	60/14		
tomato	70	✔	-	-	-	-	-	-	40/10		
medium apple	170	-	✔	-	-	-	-	-	325/77		

| Day Mon.

Date 15 Jan.

Food item | Portion (g or ml) | Food variety* | | | | | | | Food (kJ/ Cal) | Exer- cise (kJ/ Cal) | Triggers to eating |
		Vegetables, legumes	Fruit	Bread, cereals	Milk, dairy	Meat, fish, eggs, nuts	Fats	Other			
Snack 1 slice rye bread	37	-	-	✔	-	-	-	-	375/89		hunger
1 tsp vegemite	5	-	-	-	-	-	-	✔	30/7		
cheese (reduced-fat)	15	-	-	-	✔	-	-	-	250/60		
Dinner chicken & veg. lasagna	100	✔	-	✔	-	✔	-	-	420/100	brisk walk to shop and back (20 min.)	social : eating with family but not hungry
baked potato (no fat)	100	✔	-	-	-	-	-	-	305/73		
2 tbsp boiled pumpkin	100	✔	-	-	-	-	-	-	195/46		
10 pds boiled snow peas	30	✔	-	-	-	-	-	-	45/11		
1 cup garden salad	180	✔	-	-	-	-	-	-	290/70		
low-fat dressing	20	-	-	-	-	-	-	✔	160/40		
1 kiwi fruit	80	-	✔	-	-	-	-	-	160/40		
yoghurt (diet lite)	100	-	-	-	✔	-	-	-	190/46	560/ 130	
low-joule jelly	200	-	-	-	-	-	-	✔	30/8		
Snack 1 cup pop-corn (reg.)	8	-	-	✔	-	-	-	-	155/37		boredom
Total		7	5	7	4	3	1	5	6250/ 1500	1400/ 330	

*Aim for the following intake daily:
- at least 5–7 portions vegetables/legumes
- at least 2–4 portions fruit
- at least 5–7 portions bread/breakfast cereal/rice/pasta (preferably wholegrain)
- 2–4 portions milk/dairy products
- 2–4 portions meat/fish/eggs/nuts
- 1 portion fat (preferably mono-unsaturated).

RECOMMENDED FOOD-ENERGY INTAKES

Everybody is different and so are energy needs. There are variations even among people of the same age, sex, weight, height and pattern of activity. The table below provides a guide to the range of kilojoules required daily by women and men, according to age, weight and height. Remember that to change kilojoules to calories you divide by 4.184 (dividing by 4.2 gives a reasonably accurate value).

Recommended daily food-energy intake (kJ)

weight (kg)	height (cm)	18–30 years	30–60 years	over 60 years
WOMEN				
51	150	7200 – 8300	7200 – 8300	6500 – 7500
58	160	7900 – 9000	7700 – 8800	6900 – 7900
65	170	8500 – 9700	8000 – 9200	7300 – 8400
73	180	9200 – 10,500	8400 – 9600	7700 – 8800
81	190	9900 – 11,300	8800 – 10,100	8200 – 9300
MEN				
58	160	9100 – 10,400	9000 – 10,300	7400 – 8500
65	170	9800 – 11,200	9500 – 10,800	7900 – 9000
73	180	10,500 – 12,000	10,000 – 11,400	8400 – 9600
81	190	11,200 – 12,800	10,600 – 12,100	9000 – 10,300
90	200	12,000 – 13,700	11,200 – 12,800	9600 – 11,000

Adapted from *Dietary Allowances for Use in Australia*, National Health and Medical Research Council.

Adjusting your intake

The table above is for a range of activity: from people in sedentary occupations to people carrying out general household duties (including the care of small children) or light industrial work. It includes occasional activities such as gardening and non-strenuous sports.

The table below shows how to adjust your intake if your activity level does not fall within this range. Here are general guidelines.

- If you are **inactive** (for example bedridden), kilojoules must be *subtracted*.
- If you undertake regular and prolonged **moderate activity** (for example physical labour, social sports, cycling, tennis, cricket, dancing), kilojoules must be *added*.
- If you undertake regular and prolonged **strenuous activity** (for example activity that leads to sweating – heavy physical labour, vigorous sports, jogging), kilojoules must be *added*.
- When you are **pregnant** or **breastfeeding**, kilojoules must be *added*.

Daily kilojoule/calorie adjustments for different types of activity

Weight (kg)	INACTIVITY Subtract (kJ/Cal)	MODERATE ACTIVITY Add (kJ/Cal)	STRENUOUS ACTIVITY Add (kJ/Cal)
41 – 50	– 2000/480	+ 1000/240	+ 2000/480
51 – 60	– 2400/570	+ 1200/290	+ 2400/570
61 – 70	– 2800/670	+ 1400/330	+ 2800/670
71 – 80	– 3200/760	+ 1600/380	+ 3200/770
81 – 90	– 3600/860	+ 1800/430	+ 3600/860

In the second and third trimesters of pregnancy, add 590–1100 kJ (140–260 Cal) per day. When breastfeeding, add 1800–3770 kJ(450–900 Cal) per day, depending on level of milk produced.

Adapted from *Dietary Allowances for Use in Australia*, National Health and Medical Research Council.

WHY IS EXERCISE ESSENTIAL?

Physical exercise is necessary for everyone for general fitness and good health. The health benefits of exercise are well documented and include:

- improved muscle tone and circulation
- reduced stress and blood pressure
- reduced risk of heart disease
- better posture
- raised self-esteem and sense of well-being.

In addition to these considerable health benefits exercise helps regulate your appetite, and increase your metabolism so that you will burn fat for several hours after you've stopped exercising. If you have been on and off strict weight-reducing diets for many years, your metabolism slows down – sometimes by as much as 20 per cent. In this situation exercise gives the metabolic engine the kick it needs.

Exercise is particularly important for anyone wanting to lose weight and *keep it off*. Be aware that you will lose weight if you use more energy than you taken in through eating and drinking. So you should aim to eat less than you normally do and at the same time use more energy by exercising more.

GETTING IN THE EXERCISE

You may find it hard to fit in an exercise programme, but don't be put off: every extra activity helps. Try the following tips.

- Choose an exercise that you enjoy or are good at.
- Develop an active frame of mind ('I'm an active person. I'm doing something that is good for me').
- Schedule your exercise – if you decide that you will exercise when you have the time, you never will.

- Exercise at least three sessions a week to reap the metabolism-boosting benefits.
- Exercise at least 20 but preferably 30–45 minutes each session. Start with 10–20 minutes and work up slowly.
- Exercise realistically. This is crucial. Set realistic goals. Avoid an all-or-nothing attitude to exercise.
- Don't overdo it. If you are tired, slow down or stop; healthy exercise means no pain, no discomfort, and no distress. Make sure you observe rest days, especially if you are exercising hard.
- Don't make a plan that depends entirely on favourable weather – have exercise tapes or videos for hot or rainy days.
- Don't feel guilty if you miss one or two sessions, but don't use this as an excuse to give up.
- Seek motivation from family, friends or a group.
- Keep a chart (see below). It's another great motivator – *maintaining motivation is the basic principle*.

Exercise Chart

Day	Type of exercise	Duration	kJ/Cal used in exercise	How do I feel?
Sun.				
Mon.				
Tues.				
Wed.				
Thurs.				
Fri.				
Sat.				
Total (duration and kJ/Cal.)				

The chart on this page shows you how sport and leisure activities can help you control your weight.

Ten ways to work off the weight

Type of activity	Duration	Rate/Intensity	Times a week	Total food energy used per week	
				kJ	Cal
Walking	30 min.	brisk, approx. 5.5 km/h	6	4890	1170
Cycling	1 hour	approx. 20 km/h	3	4020	960
Jogging	1 hour	approx. 10 km/h	3	4510	1080
Swimming	30 min.	leisurely	4	4180	1000
Horseriding	1 hour	mainly trotting	3	4510	1080
Racquet sports	45 min.	singles	3	3950	945
Dancing	1 hour	jazz/disco	3	4640	1110
Aerobics	30 min.	step/advanced	3	4890	1170
	45 min.	light/aquarobics	3	4510	1080
Skiing	1 hour	downhill	3	4680	1120
Hiking	2 hours	9 kg backpack, 5–6 km/h	1	2540	610

Remember :

- ■ warm up with stretching activities before you start exercising
- ■ consult your doctor before you start any exercise regime, particularly if you have a strong family history of heart disease, a high cholesterol level, you are 10% overweight, a heavy smoker, or have chronic health problems
- ■ consider visiting a physical educator, even just once, to plan an exercise programme tailored to your needs and level of fitness.

Sample exercise plan

Personal details : Carol M.

- Thirty-six years old, mother of two children, wants to lose weight (about 6 kg), increase her energy level and reduce stress.
- Has a sedentary part-time job, no sporting history and has been assessed by her doctor to be in generally good health.
- Average daily food-energy intake is 9200 kJ (2200 Cal).

Short-term goals: Thinking positively about being active; incorporate exercise into lifestyle; cut fat intake and stick to a sensible eating plan (6250kJ/1500 Cal).

Long-term goals: Improve aerobic fitness, strength and energy levels; reduce stress levels and feel better about self; lose 6 kg over 12–15 weeks.

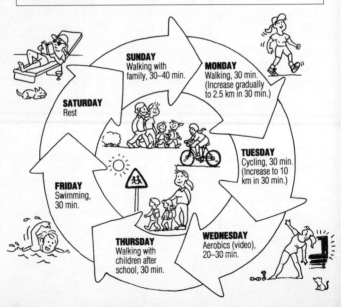

SUNDAY
Walking with family, 30–40 min.

MONDAY
Walking, 30 min. (Increase gradually to 2.5 km in 30 min.)

SATURDAY
Rest

TUESDAY
Cycling, 30 min. (Increase to 10 km in 30 min.)

FRIDAY
Swimming, 30 min.

WEDNESDAY
Aerobics (video), 20–30 min.

THURSDAY
Walking with children after school, 30 min.

USING A WEIGHT-CHANGE CHART

Each week record how much weight you have lost or gained, using the chart below. Avoid weighing yourself more than once a week.

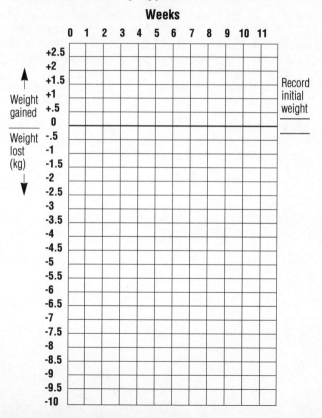

MAINTAINING YOUR DESIRABLE WEIGHT

Once you have achieved your goal of losing weight, here are some
tips.

- Gradually add foods back into your diet so that you don't go
  on losing weight. The best choices are extra bread (watch
  the toppers), cereal, fruit, vegetables and other items from the
  five basic food groups. Favourite or indulgence foods may also
  be included occasionally.
- Weigh yourself once a week (not more often) and record the
  result, to check that your weight remains constant (give or take
  1.0 – 1.5 kg).
- Try not to think like a dieting person. Listen to your body cues
  and eat when you're hungry and stop when you begin to feel
  full. Make exercise a part of your life.

ALCOHOL

Alcohol provides energy at 29 kilojoules (7 calories) per gram, but alcoholic beverages provide few other nutrients. You should therefore avoid or strictly limit them if you are trying to lose weight.

ALCOHOL AND HEALTH

In high daily doses (see 'How much is safe?', p. 31) alcohol is toxic, damaging the liver, the pancreas and the nervous system. It also alters the way the stomach and the bowel work.

Drinking too much can lead to poor nutrition, both because eating patterns may change and because the absorption of nutrients is affected by alcohol damage to the pancreas and the liver. This in turn leads to a number of other health problems.

The picture for cardiovascular health is not clear-cut. Moderate to heavy consumption of alcohol appears to lead to high blood pressure and heart-muscle damage, and heavy drinkers appear to have a greater risk of coronary heart disease. At the same time there is some evidence to suggest that *very* moderate regular drinkers (see 'How much is safe?', p. 31) may have a lower risk of coronary heart disease than either heavy drinkers or non-drinkers.

Alcoholism describes the condition of a person's becoming dependent on a high daily consumption of alcohol and being unable to limit drinking without the aid of therapy. As well as being responsible for the progressive effects of poor eating patterns and damage to organs of the body, alcoholism is strongly linked to cancers of the head, neck, oesophagus, liver and colon. It also affects personal relationships and job performance. Total abstinence from alcohol is recommended for people with alcoholism.

ALCOHOL AND PREGNANCY

Drinking alcohol during pregnancy increases the risk of foetal abnormalities. Heavy drinking may cause the infant to be born with various developmental abnormalities, including a small head, a characteristic facial appearance, or mental retardation.

Health authorities recommend that you avoid alcohol while you are pregnant.

ALCOHOL AND ROAD SAFETY

Safety on our roads and current drink-driving laws mean that you must be particularly aware of your alcohol consumption when you intend to drive. The alcohol table on p. 33 and the information below will give you the details you need to know for safety and to make sure that your alcohol consumption stays within legal limits, that is, enabling you to have a blood-alcohol reading of less than .05.

THE STANDARD DRINK

The standard drink is the volume that contains approximately 8–10 grams of alcohol:

- 375 ml of low-alcohol beer
- 250 ml standard beer
- 100 ml wine (red or white)
- 60 ml sherry or port
- 30 ml spirits.

It is important to remember that the standard drink isn't necessarily the same as the usual serving size (see the alcohol table on p. 33).

HOW MUCH IS SAFE?

Recommended 'safe' limits vary — from person to person, and according to the hazard you are considering and your sex.

- Because of physiological differences and generally lower blood volumes, 'safe' levels are lower for females than for males.
- One to two standard drinks per day for women, and up to four for men, is consistent with the Dietary Guidelines.
- In relation to cardiovascular health, one standard drink per day for women, and two for men, might be described as 'very moderate' (see 'Alcohol and health', p. 29).
- In relation to general health, more than 40 grams of alcohol per day for women and 60 grams per day for men is considered a high dose, and harmful, while less than 20 grams per day for women and less than 40 grams per day for men is considered safe.

- For pregnant women, and for people suffering from alcoholism, the safe level is zero.
- Road traffic authorities advise that the safest blood-alcohol count for drivers is zero. Staying within the legal limit of .05 entails having not more than one standard drink per hour for men and less than one for women.

HOW TO REDUCE YOUR INTAKE

If you are used to drinking alcohol, try the following:

- choose low-alcohol drinks, especially light beer
- make longer drinks by adding more ice and more mixers to spirits, or by adding fruit juice, water or ice to wine.
- don't top up your glass
- drink alcohol less often, using mineral water, ice water or fruit juice as substitutes
- as a long-term measure, modify your social habits so that alcohol is not the focus.

THE ALCOHOL TABLE

The table on p. 33 sets out the alcohol content of a range of drinks. Included are figures for low-alcohol beers and low-alcohol chardonnay. Use this information to monitor the amount of alcohol you consume; use the Counter for the kilojoule or calorie value of individual drinks.

ALCOHOL

	g/100ml	ml standard drink	av g/standard drink
beer	3.9	glass 250	10
		can 375	15
extra light	less than 1	glass 250	2
low-alcohol (light)	1.6–2.6	glass 250	5
		can 375	8
cider ... dry	3.8	250	10
sweet	3.7	250	9.5
liqueurs ... advocaat	12.8	30	4
cherry brandy	19	30	7
curacao	29.3	30	10
port	15.9	60	10
sherry ... dry	15.7	60	10
medium	14.8	60	9
... sweet	15.6	60	10
spirits ... 70% proof brandy/gin/rum/vodka/whisky	31.7	nip 30	9.5
stout	4.3	glass 250	11
		can 375	16
vermouth ... dry	13.9	60	8.5
sweet	13	60	8
wine ... low-alcohol chardonnay	6	100	6
red	9.5	100	10
rosé	8.7	100	9
white ... dry	9.1	100	9
medium	8.8	100	9
sparkling	9.9	100	10
sweet	10.2	100	10

THE
COUNTER

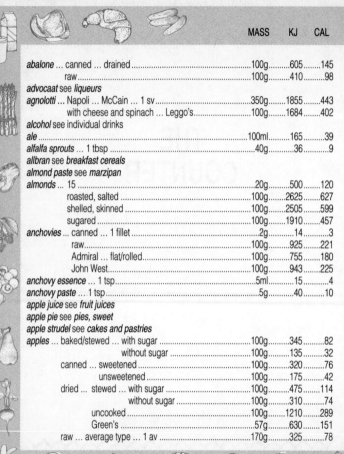

	MASS	KJ	CAL
abalone ... canned ... drained	100g	605	145
raw	100g	410	98
advocaat see *liqueurs*			
agnolotti ... Napoli ... McCain ... 1 sv	350g	1855	443
with cheese and spinach ... Leggo's	100g	1684	402
alcohol see individual drinks			
ale	100ml	165	39
alfalfa sprouts ... 1 tbsp	40g	36	9
allbran see *breakfast cereals*			
almond paste see *marzipan*			
almonds ... 15	20g	500	120
roasted, salted	100g	2625	627
shelled, skinned	100g	2505	599
sugared	100g	1910	457
anchovies ... canned ... 1 fillet	2g	14	3
raw	100g	925	221
Admiral ... flat/rolled	100g	755	180
John West	100g	943	225
anchovy essence ... 1 tsp	5ml	15	4
anchovy paste ... 1 tsp	5g	40	10
apple juice see *fruit juices*			
apple pie see *pies, sweet*			
apple strudel see *cakes and pastries*			
apples ... baked/stewed ... with sugar	100g	345	82
without sugar	100g	135	32
canned ... sweetened	100g	320	76
unsweetened	100g	175	42
dried ... stewed ... with sugar	100g	475	114
without sugar	100g	310	74
uncooked	100g	1210	289
Green's	57g	630	151
raw ... average type ... 1 av	170g	325	78

	MASS	KJ	CAL
Delicious ... 1 av	185g	390	93
Golden Delicious ... 1 av	135g	225	54
Granny Smith ... 1 av	179g	285	68
Jonathan ... 1 av	125g	235	56
apricot chicken ... Healthy Choice ... 1 sv	280g	1254	300
apricot nectar ... canned	100g	250	60
apricots ... canned ... in pear juice ... 3 halves + 35ml juice	85g	150	36
drained ... 1 cup	220g	375	90
in syrup ... 1 cup	260g	570	136
drained ... 3 halves	50g	105	25
artific. sweet. ... 3 halves + 40ml liquid	90g	90	22
unsweetened	100g	140	33
dried ... stewed ... with sugar	100g	510	122
without sugar	100g	350	84
uncooked ... ½	4g	45	11
raw ... 1 av	60g	85	20
stewed ... with sugar	100g	350	84
without sugar	100g	90	22
Goulburn Valley ... in fruit juice	100g	198	47
SPC ... in syrup	100g	250	60
just fruit	100g	219	52
nutradiet ... artific. sweet.	100g	120	29
snak pak ... in juice	140g	305	73
in syrup	140g	340	81

D ried apricots are a good source of dietary fibre as well as B carotene. For those with a sweet tooth, dried fruit is preferable to sweets.

	MASS	KJ	CAL
Weight Watchers	100g	125	30
arrowroot	100g	1445	345
artichoke hearts ... Admiral	100g	55	13
artichoke, globe ... boiled ... inner leaves + base ... 1	120g	105	25
artichoke, Jerusalem ... boiled ... peeled ... 1	320g	330	79
asparagus ... boiled ... 5 spears	70g	55	13
Edgell	100g	101	24
Farmland/John West	100g	100	24
SPC	100g	75	18
asparagus rolls ... 1 av	45g	185	44
aubergine see *eggplant*			
avocado ... raw ... flesh only ... ½	121g	1065	255
baba ghannouj see *dips and spreads*			
babaco ... raw ... peeled ... flesh only ... ¼	277g	225	54
bacon ... fried ... medium fat ... 1 rasher	34g	530	127
grilled ... medium fat ... 1 rasher	30g	405	97
bacon burger ... frozen ... fried ... av all brands	100g	1040	249
crumbed ... av all brands	100g	1535	367
grilled ... av all brands	100g	1050	251
crumbed ... av all brands	100g	1455	348
Baron's Table ... 1 sv	50g	305	73
bagels ... 1	85g	950	227
Sara Lee ... plain ... 1	85g	800	191
baked beans ... Edgell	100g	433	103
Farmland ... no added salt	100g	420	100
SPC	100g	390	93
baked beans in barbecue sauce ... Heinz ... 1 sv	100g	470	112
baked beans in ham sauce ... Heinz ... 1 sv	100g	465	111

Grill bacon until crisp and most of the fat will run off and can be discarded. A 75 g rasher can reduce from 1340 kJ (320 Cal) to around 715 kJ (170 Cal).

	MASS	KJ	CAL
baked beans in tomato sauce/salt-reduced ... Heinz	100g	385	92
baked beans plus ... Heinz ... av all styles ...1 sv	100g	430	103
baklava see *cakes and pastries*			
balance oat bran see *breakfast cereals*			
bamboo shoots ... raw	20g	25	6
Admiral	100g	140	33
banana custard see *custard, banana*			
bananas ... common variety ... raw ... peeled ... flesh only ... 1	140g	500	120
sugar/lady finger ... raw ... peeled ... flesh only ... 1	60g	265	63
baps ... 1	65g	645	154
barbecue sauce see *sauces, savoury*			
barley, pearl ... boiled ... 1 tbsp	10g	45	11
dried ... uncooked ... 1 tbsp	15g	190	45
barramundi ... baked	100g	410	98
battered, fried	100g	835	200
grilled	100g	400	96
poached	100g	395	94
poached/grilled ... no fat	100g	395	94
raw	100g	320	76
smoked	100g	335	80
steamed	100g	350	84
bean sprouts ... raw ... 1 cup	90g	75	18
Admiral	100g	145	35
beans ... McCain ... whole baby/golden	100g	131	31
beans, blackeye ... dried	100g	1425	341
beans, broad ... fresh ... boiled ... 1 cup	170g	295	71
raw ... beans from 10 pods	92g	160	38
Edgell	100g	208	50
beans, butter ... boiled ... 1 cup sliced	140g	115	27
cooked, cannellini style	100g	515	123
frozen ... boiled	100g	130	31
raw ... 10 beans	77g	65	16

	MASS	KJ	CAL
Edgell	100g	393	94
cannellini style/ golden butter-beans	100g	350	84
beans, green ... canned...drained ... 1 cup	230g	230	55
dried...boiled ... 1 cup	115g	135	32
fresh...boiled ... 1 cup	140g	95	23
frozen....boiled ... 1 cup	125g	95	23
raw ... 1 cup sliced	120g	105	25
Birds Eye ... cross-cut/sliced/frozen	100g	142	34
Golden Circle ... av all brands ... sliced	100g	135	32
beans, haricot (navy) ... boiled	100g	380	91
beans, lima ... dried ... boiled	100g	300	72
raw	100g	1420	339
Sanitarium ... ¼ can	110g	374	89
beans, mixed ... dried ... average type	100g	1450	347
cooked ... average type	100g	525	125
Edgell/Masterfoods	100g	406	97
beans, mung ... cooked (dahl)	100g	350	84
dried ... raw	100g	1430	342
raw	100g	980	234
sprouts ... canned	100g	40	10
raw	100g	145	35
beans, purple ... boiled ... 1 cup sliced	140g	170	41
raw ... 10 beans	105g	125	30
beans, red kidney ... canned ... drained ... ½ cup	100g	375	90
dried	100g	1060	253
fresh ... 1 cup	165g	790	189
Edgell	100g	396	95

Bean sprouts blanched (at only 30 kJ/7 Cal per 30 g) and added to rice can bulk out a lower-energy base for curries and kebabs, as well as adding a satisfying crunch.

	MASS	KJ	CAL
Green's	100g	380	91
Masterfoods ... drained	100g	570	136
beans, snake ... boiled ... 1 cup sliced	140g	135	32
raw ... 10 beans	120g	115	27
beans, soya ... boiled ... dried	100g	545	130
canned ... drained ... ½ cup	100g	385	92
raw ... fresh	100g	560	134
Masterfoods ... drained	100g	465	111
Sanitarium ... in tomato sauce ... ¼ can	110g	396	95
natural ... ⅛ can	72g	201	48

beef

	MASS	KJ	CAL
blade steak ... grilled ... lean ... 1 av	112g	830	198
lean + fat ... 1 av	120g	1035	247
boneless average cut ... cooked	100g	890	213
lean ... 1 cup diced	190g	1455	348
lean + fat ... 1 cup diced	182g	1805	431
brisket, corned ... boiled ... lean ... 1 slice	32g	285	68
lean + fat ... 1 slice	43g	560	184
chuck steak ... simmered ... lean ... 1 cup diced	156g	1325	317
lean + fat ... 1 cup diced	179g	1920	459
fillet steak ... grilled ... lean ... 1 av	70g	575	137
lean + fat ... 1 av	77g	750	179
heart ... simmered ... 1 cup chopped	190g	1190	284
kidney ... simmered ... 1 cup diced	150g	850	203
liver ... simmered ... 1 cup chopped	140g	1290	308
mince ... dry-fried	100g	1195	286
regular ... simmered, drained ... 1 cup	170g	1300	311
rib steak (porterhouse) ... grilled ... lean ... 1 av	103g	760	182
lean + fat ... 1 av	130g	1640	392
rib-eye steak ... grilled ... lean ... 1 av	94g	780	186
lean + fat ... 1av	108g	1160	277

	MASS	KJ	CAL
round steak ... grilled ... lean ... 1 av	249g	1840	440
lean+fat ... 1 av	265g	2250	538
rump steak ... fried ... 1 av	150g	1535	367
grilled ... lean ... 1 av	174g	1400	335
lean+fat ... 1 av	199g	2240	535
sandwich steak ... frozen ... grilled ... av all brands	100g	1425	341
silverside ... baked ... lean ... 1 slice	41g	395	94
lean+fat ... 1 slice	37g	275	66
silverside, corned ... boiled ... lean+fat ... 1 slice	45g	385	92
lean ... 1 slice	39g	210	50
sirloin roast ... 1 sv	120g	1415	338
sirloin steak ... grilled ... lean ... 1 av	104g	840	201
lean+fat ... 1 av	127g	1455	348
skirt steak ... simmered ... lean ... 1 cup diced	181g	1430	342
lean+fat ... 1 cup diced	184g	1520	363
tail ... simmered ... 1 cup	81g	1175	281
tongue ... simmered ... 1 slice	20g	260	62
topside roast ... baked ... lean ... 1 slice	41g	260	62
lean+fat ... 1 slice	45g	360	86

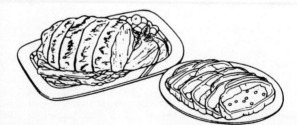

	MASS	KJ	CAL
tripe ... simmered ... 1 cup chopped	175g	610	146
beef burgers ... frozen ... fried ... 1	60g	660	158
Baron's Table ... 1	50g	230	55
Birds Eye ... crumbed	100g	1210	289
I & J ... big beefers ... 1	125g	1443	345
lean beefers ... 1	67g	466	111
l'il beefers ... 1	50g	577	138
beef casserole ... 1 sv	180g	945	226
with vegetables ... (chuck steak)	100g	710	170
without vegetables ... (chuck steak)	100g	745	178
beef chow mein (Chinese)	100g	580	139
beef curry ... canned ... av commercial brands	100g	765	183
Kraft ... snack pack	100g	690	165
Vesta ... 1 pkt made up ... 2 svs	223g	3449	824
beef German see *luncheon meat*			
beef hot salad (Thai)	100g	390	93
beef in oyster sauce (Chinese)	100g	625	149
beef Italienne with tagliatelle ... Findus Lean Cuisine ... 1 sv	250g	1067	255
beef medallions ... Healthy Choice ... 1 sv	310g	1039	248
beef oriental ... Findus Lean Cuisine ... 1 sv	245g	1088	260
beef panang ... Greens	100g	516	123
beef rissoles ... 1 large	100g	1065	255
beef satay ... fresh/Farmland ... 1 sv	200g	1380	330
Healthy Choice ... 1 sv	270g	1243	297
beef satay (Chinese/Thai)	100g	805	192
beef steak and vegetables ... Kraft	100g	790	189
Farmland ... no added salt	100g	295	71

Grilling beefburgers on a wire rack until well done means that a substantial proportion of their fat can be cooked out and discarded. A 630 kJ (150 Cal) beefburger will reduce to 480 kJ (115 Cal) in this way.

	MASS	KJ	CAL
beef, corned ... canned ... with cereal ... av commercial brands	100g	825	197
Plumrose ... deli	100g	590	141
beer ... Carlton D ale	375ml	469	112
Cascade premium lager	375ml	596	142
Castlemaine DL lager	375ml	448	107
Castlemaine XXXX bitter ale/Emu bitter	375ml	574	137
Coopers DB	375ml	495	118
Fosters lager/Victoria bitter ... 1 can	375ml	600	143
Reschs pilsener	375ml	544	130
Southwark premium	375ml	690	165
Swan lager/Tooheys dry	375ml	611	146
Toohey's draught ... small bottle	375ml	577	138
West End/Boags draught/Castlemaine dry	375ml	551	132
beer, reduced alcohol ... Boags tiger head/Cascade	375ml	469	112
Carlton light	375ml	448	107
Castlemaine XL bitter/XXXX light bitter	375ml	368	88
Castlemaine XXXX gold/Swan gold	375ml	441	105
Coopers light/Tooheys lite	375ml	356	85
Fosters special bitter	375ml	488	117
Swan light	375ml	289	69
Tooheys blue	375ml	514	123
West End light	375ml	375	90
beer nuts see *snack foods*			
beetroot ... boiled ... flesh only ... 2 slices	60g	105	25
Edgell	100g	186	44
Farmland ... sliced ... no added salt	100g	195	47
Golden Circle	100g	230	55
biscuits			
anzac ... av all brands ... 1	19g	360	86
bran ... av all brands ... 1	13g	245	59
brownies/chocolate chip ... av all brands ... 1	12g	245	59

	MASS	KJ	CAL
butter ... av all brands ... 1	12g	230	55
carob ... av all brands ... 1	18g	375	90
cheese-flavoured ... av all brands ... 1	3g	60	14
cheese straws ... home-made	100g	1905	455
chocolate chip and nuts ... av all brands	9g	190	45
chocolate-coated ... av all brands ... 1	14g	280	67
cream- and/or jam-filled ... av all brands ... 1	13g	275	66
marshmallow-filled ... av all brands ... 1	23g	425	102
chocolate-flavoured ... av all brands ... 1	9g	160	38
cracker ... high-fat ... av all brands	100g	2060	492
low-fat ... av all brands	100g	1675	400
medium-fat ... av all brands	100g	1975	472
cream- and jam-filled ... av all brands ... 1	16g	330	79

Beetroot is one of the highest-fibre root vegetables you can buy and is lower in kilojoules by weight than potato. Grate raw beetroot into a salad. Boil or steam beetroot gently, or wrap it in foil and bake for 40–60 minutes, rubbing the skin off after cooking and while it is still hot. If you have a microwave oven you only need to twist the leafy tops off the beetroot. Avoid piercing the skin and try to leave 3–5 cm of root at the base of the vegetable. Microwave on HIGH for 8 minutes per 250 g. Beetroot is simply delicious with a low-fat yoghurt and chive topping, or served as a side salad sprinkled with a little vinegar.

	MASS	KJ	CAL
cream-filled ... av all flavours ... av all brands ... 1	15g	295	71
crispbread ... rye ... av all brands	100g	1505	360
wheat ... av all brands	100g	1735	415
fruit ... av all brands ... 1	10g	190	45
fruit and nuts ... av all brands ... 1	10g	205	49
fruit-filled ... av all brands ... 1	15g	250	60
fruit, iced ... av all brands ... 1	12g	245	59
ginger ... av all brands ... 1	13g	220	53
iced ... av all brands ... 1	11g	190	45
jam-filled ... av all brands ... 1	13g	225	54
macaroons ... av all brands ... 1	10g	200	48
marshmallow ... av all brands ... 1	17g	280	67
muesli bars see *health-food bars*			
nuts ... av all brands ... 1	11g	225	54
oatmeal ... av all brands ... 1	10g	195	47
plain ... av all brands ... 1	6g	110	26
salted ... av all brands ... 1	3g	60	14
sweet ... av all brands ... 1	8g	155	37
polyunsaturated ... *sweet* ... av all brands ... 1	14g	250	60
puffed and toasted/extra-fibre ... av all brands ... 1	5g	80	19
rye ... av all brands ... 1	8g	105	25
savoury-flavoured ... av all brands ... 1	2g	40	10
shortbread ... av all brands ... 1	12g	240	57
starch-reduced ... av all brands ... 1	7g	120	29
wafers (filled) ... av all brands ... 1	7g	155	37
water crackers ... av all brands ... 1	4g	65	16
wheatmeal ... av all brands ... 1	9g	165	39
wholewheat ... av all brands ... 1	5g	90	22
wholewheat and sesame ... av all brands ... 1	5g	90	22
Arnotts ... Cheds ... 1		160	38
Chocolate Cavetto ... 1		330	79

	MASS	KJ	CAL
Choc Fruit and Nut/Choc Gaiety ... 1		280	67
Choc Mint Slice/Choc Caramel Crowns ... 1		360	86
Chocolate Ripple/Tea Cake ... 1		180	43
Chocolate Royals/Chocolate Dessert Cream/ Creamy Choc ... 1		305	73
Choc Teddy Bear/Choc Duet ... 1		345	82
Chocolate Tee Vee Snacks ... 1		110	26
Chocolate Tim Tam/Choc Cherry Crown ... 1		415	99
Clix ... 1		65	16
Cruskits ... Bran and Malt/Rye ... 1		75	17
Plain ... 1		120	29
Farmbake Choc Chip/Peanut Brownies ... 1		245	59
Granita/Butternut Snap/Arno Shortbread... 1		250	60
Hundreds and Thousands/Iced Tic Toc/ Honey Jumble ... 1		180	43
Malt O Milk/Arrowroot/Honey Snap ... 1		140	33
Monte Carlo ... 1		420	100
Nice/Maryland/Oatables ... 1		230	55
Nik Nax ... all varieties ... 1		20	5
Raisin Luncheon ... 1		200	48
Raspberry Tartlets/Iced Vo Vo ... 1		250	60
Salada ... all varieties ... 1 quarter		56	13
Sao ... 1		160	38
Savoy ... 1		85	20
Scotch Finger ... 1		360	86
Shapes, Savoury-flavoured/Cheese/Cheddar ... 1		40	10
Shortbread Cream ... 1		390	83
Venetian/Date Bar/Raspberry Shortcake ... 1		275	65
Vita Weat ... all varieties ...1		95	23
Water Cracker ... all varieties ... 1		50	12
Cadbury ... chocolate/caramel wafers ...1		285	68

	MASS	KJ	CAL
chocolate doubles ... 1		445	106
clovers ... 1		263	63
toffee pops/squiggle tops ...1		343	82
zoo animals ... 1 av		112	27
Cereal Foods ... captains table water cracker ... 1		70	17
coconut fingers/striped shortbread ... 1		290	69
coffee scrolls/honey bran and yoghurt ... 1		243	58
dixie drumsticks ... 1		40	10
garlic in a biskit ... 1		20	5
hazelnut slice/lamington ... 1		303	72
heydays ... 1		405	96
premium ... 1		65	16
savoury in a biskit/chicken in a biskit ... 1		40	10
Clarke's ... carob dipped bran treats/golden crunch ... 1		365	87
choc chip ripples ... 1		632	151
classic Dutch speculaas ... 1		320	76
classic honey butter fingers ... 1		238	57
classic royal shortbread ... 1		345	82
petticoat tails/raisin and sesame low cholesterol ... 1		283	68
Country Harvest ... caro cookies ... gluten-free	100g	2255	539
choc cookies ... gluten-free	100g	2160	516
Farmland ... choc almond/currant cookies ... 1		365	87
choc chip cookies/mocca supreme/ shortbread delight ... 1		370	88
golden snap cookies ... 1		320	76
hazelnut crunch cookies ... 1		355	85
orange and lemon crunch cookies ... 1		335	80
rich Viennese cookies ... 1		385	92
Green's ... chocolate chip cookies ... 1	12g	190	45
Limmits ... apricot and almond munch ... per meal		1093	261
cheese on wheat/choc nut/ roast chicken and herb ... per meal		1171	280

	MASS	KJ	CAL
cheese and chives on multigrain... per meal	1228	293	
choc hazelnut oat ... per meal	1212	290	
mint chocolate slice ... per meal	1330	318	
sultana munch ... per meal	1114	266	
Naytura ... almond and sesame low-cholesterol ... 1	305	73	
carob-coated bran/muesli ... 1	365	87	
gluten-free ... 1	280	67	
Players ... choc chip cookies ... 1	551	132	
choc chunk/double choc ... 1	999	239	
choc teddy/mini mates/swissh ... 1	521	124	
Premier Japan ... rice crackers ... 1	60	14	
Sunshine ... choc galore ... 1	275	66	
cream treats/lemon cream/orange cream ... 1	355	85	
custard cream ... 1	365	87	
ginger crunch ... 1	110	26	
marie/milk coffee ... 1	155	37	
nice/shortbread treats ... 1	175	42	
orange crunch ... 1	210	50	
Westons ... choc chip cookies ... 1	235	56	
chocolate wheaten ... 1	485	116	
crackerbread/macaroon delights ... 1	95	23	
jam fancies ... 1	260	62	
marie/scotch fingers ... 1	180	43	
roundabouts ... 1	345	82	
snowballs ... 1	245	59	
strawberry mallows ... 1	160	38	
ryvita ... 1	126	30	
wagon wheels ... 1	816	195	
Willow Valley ... oat bran with choc chips ... 1	565	135	
with fruit and nuts ... 1	600	143	
***black pudding (sausage)* ... av commercial brands**	100g	1080	258

	MASS	KJ	CAL
blackberries ... canned ... sweetened	100g	300	72
unsweetened	100g	165	39
raw	100g	245	59
stewed ... with sugar	100g	255	61
without sugar	100g	125	30
blackcurrants ... raw	100g	245	59
blueberries ... John West ... canned in syrup	100g	291	69
bogong moth ... abdomen	100g	1910	455
bonox ... Kraft ... 1 tsp	8g	31	7
Boston bun see *buns*			
bourghul ... dried ... Lowan Whole Foods	100g	1480	354
see also *bulgur*			
brains see *lamb; veal*			
braised beef steak ... canned	100g	885	211
braised beef steak and onions ... canned ... av all brands	100g	715	170
bran see *breakfast cereals*			
brandy see *spirits*			
brazil nuts ... shelled ... snack-size	50g	1335	317
bread			
flat breads ... chapati ... +fat ... 1	100g	1385	331

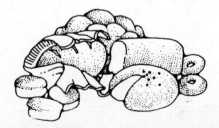

	MASS	KJ	CAL
no fat ... 1	100g	860	206
Lebanese ... white ... 24 cm diam ... 1	110g	1234	295
wholemeal ... 24 cm diam ... 1	110g	1086	260
matzo ... 1	30g	490	117
pita ... Oasis ... 1	80g	860	206
with oat fibre ... 1	75g	780	186
Tip Top ... Egyptian ... white ... 1	65g	705	168
wholemeal ... 1	65g	699	167
pocket ... white/wholemeal ... 1	45g	510	122
sorj ... 1	100g	1205	288
loaves ... brown sandwich ... 1 slice	28g	270	65
toasted ... 1 slice	23g	265	63
fruit bread ... brown ... heavy ... 1 slice	45g	535	128
continental fruit ... 1 slice	20g	205	49
white ... light ... 1 slice	30g	305	73
pumpernickel ... 1 slice	60g	460	110
raisin ... 1 slice	60g	655	157
rye ... dark ... 1 slice	50g	425	102
light ... 1 slice	37g	375	90
starch-reduced ... 1 slice	20g	205	49
Vienna ... 1 slice	30g	310	74
white ... high-fibre ... toasted ... 1 slice	23g	265	63
sandwich ... 1 slice	28g	290	69

Eating Too Little Can Hinder Weight Loss

A diet of 3350 kJ (800 Cal) a day reduces the possibility that the body will obtain the wide range of nutrients it requires, and actually constitutes a kind of 'famine' intake because the quantity of kilojoules is inadequate. Over a long period, inadequate energy intake has the effect of making the body feel that famine is imminent, so that it strenuously resists further weight loss.

	MASS	KJ	CAL
toasted ... 1 slice	23g	285	68
wholemeal sandwich ... 1 slice	28g	290	69
1 toast-size-slice	33g	310	74
Buttercup ... country split white (450-g loaf) ... 1 slice	24g	274	65
gold medal 'oat bran' ... 1 slice	29g	307	73
golden bake multi-grain ... 1 slice		255	61
golden bake white ... 1 slice	22g	235	56
multi-grain plus ... 1 slice	29g	295	71
multi-grain plus toast ... 1 slice	34g	340	81
Pritikin whole wheat salt-reduced ... 1 slice	29g	304	73
Riga oatmeal salt-free ... 1 slice	29g	300	72
Super sandwich maker ... 1 slice	29g	313	75
toasty ... 1 slice	34g	361	86
wholemeal plus toast ... 1 slice	34g	348	83
wonder white ... 2 slices	65g	687	164
Sunicrust ... suni-sandwich ... white/wholemeal ... 1 slice	29g	303	72
suni-toast ... hi-fibre white ... 1 slice	35g	353	84
wholemeal ... 1 slice	35g	368	88
suni-treats raisin bread ... 1 slice	32g	398	95
suni-wholegrain ... 1 slice	32g	342	82
suni-7-grains ... 1 slice	29g	313	75
Taylors ... wholemeal ... 1 slice	45g	475	114
Tip Top ... mighty white ... 1 slice	31g	334	80
multigrain ... 1 slice	30g	305	73
spicy fruit ... 1 slice	27g	299	71
sunblest ... 1 slice	30g	307	73
weight watchers ... white ... 1 slice	20g	211	50
white hyfibe/wholemeal ... 1 slice	30g	298	71
Vogel ... wholemeal and sesame ... 1 slice	39g	396	95
Weight Watchers ... av all types ... 1 slice		190	45

	MASS	KJ	CAL
rolls ... cheese ... 1	65g	710	170
dinner ... 1	30g	300	72
hamburger ... 1	65g	645	154
horseshoe/knot/mixed-grain/torpedo ... 1	60g	595	142
sticks ... French bread stick ... 1 slice	20g	200	48
garlic bread ... 2 slices	67g	1140	272
grissini ... 2 sticks	20g	300	72
wholemeal ... 1 slice	25g	250	60
see also *bagels; baps; buns; croissants; crumpets; muffins*			
breadcrumbs ... commercial ... dried ... 2 tbsp	12g	178	42
bread mix ... gluten-free ... Country Harvest ... made up	100g	955	228
high-fibre made up	100g	885	212
multi-mix made up	100g	945	226
breadfruit ... canned ... drained	100g	275	66
raw	100g	445	106
breakfast cereals* ...			
baby cereal ... 1 bowl	30g	225	54
bran flakes ... 1 cup	45g	618	148

* One serve of average-type ready-to-eat breakfast cereal equals approximately 30 g.

Don't Skip Breakfast

Missing breakfast can mean burning almost 6 per cent fewer kilojoules during the day. Most of the kilojoules we use each day are to maintain the body's metabolic rate, which is increased by eating breakfast after we've slept. A good breakfast should supply at least 10 per cent of the day's energy intake to stimulate the metabolism for the whole day. Without breakfast our metabolism slows down and we burn fewer kilojoules.

Another danger allied to skipping breakfast is the temptation to snack during the morning on foods that will not provide the same nutrients that can be gained from a good breakfast. It may also be more difficult to control your kilojoule intake.

	MASS	KJ	CAL
bran, rice ... 1 tbsp	8g	144	34
bran, wheat ... 1 tbsp	5g	33	8
muesli ... Swiss-style ... ½ cup	65g	920	220
toasted ... ½ cup	55g	930	222
oatmeal ... boiled ... 1 cup	260g	550	131
dry ... raw ... ½ cup	48g	735	176
oats ... rolled ... boiled ... 1 cup	260g	550	131
puffed corn/puffed rice ... 1 bowl	30g	135	32
puffed wheat ... 1 cup	12g	180	43
rice bubbles ... 1 cup	30g	445	106
semolina ... cooked ... 1 cup	200g	260	62
Fountain ... raw	30g	450	108
wheatgerm ... 1 tbsp	6g	67	16
Abundant Earth ... corn/rice ... 1 sv	14g	225	54
gluten-free muesli ... 1 sv	30g	455	109
millet/wheat ... 1 sv	14g	210	50
Alevita ... muesli with fruit ... no added sugar	30g	420	100
Anchor ... oatbran	30g	480	115
Arrowhead Mills ... oatbran flakes	30g	460	110
Cerola ... toasted muesli/apricot toasted muesli	30g	510	122
Light 'n' Crunchy	30g	485	116
natural muesli	30g	475	114
Farmland ... minute oats	30g	460	110
toasted muesli	30g	580	139
Green's ... natural bran	30g	135	32
oat bran	30g	270	65
Home Brand ... fruit rings/rice puffs	30g	490	117
John Bull ... rolled oats	30g	462	110
Kellogg's ... all-bran	30g	443	106
balance oat bran	30g	791	189
corn flakes/whole wheat mini-wheats	30g	456	109
froot loops	30g	486	116

	MASS	KJ	CAL
honey smacks/frosties	30g	465	111
just right/special K	30g	461	110
komplete natural muesli/crunchy nut flakes	30g	472	113
rice bubbles/sultana bran	30g	449	107
sustain/puffed wheat	30g	483	115
toasted muesli	30g	545	130
Lowan Whole Foods ... wholegrain barley flakes/triticale flakes	30g	445	106
wholegrain wheat flakes	30g	425	102
Morning Sun ... natural muesli/peach 'n' pecan	30g	437	104
toasted tropical muesli	30g	530	127
Norco ... whey cereal delite	30g	85	20
Purina ... natural bran	30g	270	65
processed bran	30g	330	79
Swiss formula muesli/toasted muesli flakes	30g	455	109
toasted muesli	30g	560	134
Quaker ... instant porridge ... 1 sachet	34g	527	126
Sanitarium ... bran bix ... 2 biscuits	30g	370	88
bran cereal	30g	336	80
cornflakes/puffed wheat/unsweetened muesli	30g	456	109
goodstart ... 2 biscuits	40g	608	145
honey weets	30g	462	110

	MASS	KJ	CAL
toasted muesli	30g	582	139
weet-bix ... 2 biscuits	30g	420	100
weet-bix hi-bran ... 2 biscuits	40g	552	132
wheat flakes	30g	432	103
wheat germ (betta B) ... 2 tbsp	15g	213	51
Sunfarm... four brans ... 1 tbsp	15g	258	62
only natural breakfast crunch ... 1 sv	60g	1000	239
ricebran ... 1 tbsp	15g	276	66
The Old Grain Mill ... fruit and nut muesli	30g	520	124
natural bran	30g	280	67
natural muesli	30g	445	106
natural oatbran/natural wheatgerm	30g	475	114
quick-cooking oats/ rolled oats	30g	485	116
Uncle Toby's ... 1-min oats/instant porridge ... ⅓ cup ... dry	30g	465	111
breakfast bars ... fibreplus ... 1	43g	722	173
lite start ... 1	37g	568	136
sportsplus ... 1	37g	608	145
fibreplus	45g	621	148
fruit 'n' nut weeties/muesli flakes/sportsplus	45g	663	158
instant porridge + honey/rice crispies	30g	483	115
oat flakes/wheat bites	30g	441	105
pro vita weat harts ... 1 tbsp	12g	160	38
vita brits	30g	435	104
Weight Watchers ... fruit and fibre	20g	299	71
tropicana	30g	453	108
bream ... battered, deep-fried	100g	970	232
floured, pan-fried in oil	100g	830	198
steamed	100g	580	139
broccoli ... boiled/raw	50g	50	12
Birds Eye ... in cream sauce	100g	193	46
Birds Eye/McCain	100g	120	29
brussels sprouts ... boiled ... 5	100g	105	25

	MASS	KJ	CAL
Birds Eye	100g	150	36
McCain	100g	190	45
bubble 'n' squeak ... Birds Eye	100g	400	96
buckwheat ... raw ... ½ cup	100g	1520	363
Lowan Whole Foods ... kernels	100g	1400	335
bulgur ... boiled ... 1 cup	265g	955	228
dry ... 1 cup	180g	2250	538
soaked ... 1 cup	205g	1305	312
buns ... brioche	100g	1720	411
cinnamon ... 1 medium	55g	680	163
finger	100g	1240	296
fruit (Boston/coffee scroll/currant) ... iced ... 1	76g	940	225
hot cross ... 1	90g	915	219
butter ... salted/unsalted ... av all commercial brands ... 1 tbsp	20g	610	146
Dairy Farmers	20g	606	145
reduced-fat dairy spread	20g	310	74
Devondale ... dairy extra soft ... 1 tbsp	15g	285	68
Western Star ... continental cultured unsalted	20g	616	147
light	20g	452	108
see also *margarine*			
buttermilk see *milk*			
butterscotch see *confectionery*			
cabbage rolls (Lebanese)	100g	495	118
cabbage ... Chinese ... raw ... 1 cup shredded	80g	35	8
common/savoy/white ... boiled ... 1 cup shredded	135g	90	22
raw ... 1 cup shredded	85g	60	14
mustard ... raw ... 1 cup shredded	60g	40	10
red ... boiled ... 1 cup shredded	130g	90	22
raw ... 1 cup shredded	95g	90	22

	MASS	KJ	CAL

cake and pudding mixes

	MASS	KJ	CAL
Country Harvest ... gluten-free ... cakes ... made up	100g	1810	433
puddings ... vanilla/choc ... made up	100g	665	159
Green's ... cake mix ... banana cake ... made up	50g	673	161
carrot cake ... made up	50g	977	234
chocolate cake ... made up	50g	568	136
dark chocolate/Swiss milk cake	50g	744	178
date loaf ... made up	50g	541	129
golden buttercake ... made up	50g	865	207
shake a cake ... carrot/orange	50g	669	160
chocolate	50g	625	149
dessert mix ... chocolate mousse ... made up	100g	544	130
ezi-pav ... dry mix	100g	1023	245
original cheesecake ... 1 slice	80g	1120	268
self-saucing sponge puddings ... chocolate ... made up	100g	669	160
lemon/forestberry/butterscotch ... made up	100g	607	145
White Wings			
apple and oatmeal cake/madeira cake ... made up	50g	688	164
bake o scone mix ... made up	100g	1360	325

For a lower-kilojoule treat choose light and airy cakes such as fat-free whisked sponge filled with a moist fruit puree. Manufacturers tend to whisk more air into their cakes than non-commercial cakes are likely to have, so you may often find that bought cakes have fewer kilojoules than those you can make at home.

If you have prepared or bought a special cake for a particular occasion and there are likely to be leftovers to tempt you, try cutting only as much of the cake as you think you will need and freeze the rest.

	MASS	KJ	CAL
banana cake ... made up	50g	710	170
chocolate cheese cake ... made up	80g	1180	282
chocolate sponge/lemon cake ... made up	50g	650	155
date loaf ... made up	50g	590	141
French tea cake/apple spice tea/carrot ... made up	50g	670	160
microwave moist ... chocolate chip pudding ... made up	55g	915	219
chocolate cake ... made up	50g	790	189
microwave moist self-icing cake ... banana ... made up	50g	765	183
chocolate ... made up	50g	830	198
moist orange cake/moist lemon ... made up	50g	645	154
puffin self-saucing sponge cake ... made up	100g	750	179
real fruit dessert ... av all varieties ... made up	125g	415	99
rich chocolate sponge/choc cake ... made up	50g	680	163
self-saucing sponge puddings ... av all varieties except choc ... made up	125g	1020	244
chocolate ... made up	125g	1090	261
sultana buttercake ... made up	50g	700	167
cakes and pastries			
angel-food cake	100g	1135	271
apple strudel ... 1 slice	128g	1120	268
baklava ... Greek	100g	1580	378
Lebanese	100g	2080	497
black forest cake ...1 slice	80g	1140	272
carrot cake ... 1 slice	103g	1425	341
cheesecake ... 1 slice	165g	2350	562
chocolate cake, iced ... 1 slice	55g	825	197
chocolate eclair ... 1	70g	1115	266
Christmas cake ... light	100g	1490	356

	MASS	KJ	CAL
rich	100g	1595	381
cream puffs ... with custard filling	100g	965	231
cupcake ... 1	40g	620	148
custard tart ... 1	135g	1430	342
Danish pastry ... 1	100g	1290	308
date and nut loaf ... 1	100g	1500	359
fruit cake ... boiled ... 1 slice	60g	1015	243
dark ... commercial ... 1 slice	50g	695	166
light ... commercial ... 1 slice	50g	720	172
rich ... 1 slice	85g	1145	274
wedding	100g	1485	355
fruit mince slice ... 1	150g	1870	447
galactobureko (Greek)	100g	896	214
gingerbread	100g	1330	318
jam tart ... 1	45g	670	160
kataifi (Greek)	100g	1245	298
lamington ... 1	73g	950	227
madeira cake	100g	1480	354

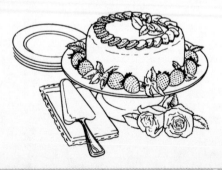

	MASS	KJ	CAL
meringue ... 1	26g	400	96
muesli slice ... 1	78g	1335	319
plain cake ... 1 slice	40g	590	141
rock cakes	100g	1670	399
sponge cake ... iced ... 1 thin slice	60g	755	180
jam + cream, not iced ... ⅛ cake	53g	715	171
sweet mince tarts	100g	1825	436
Swiss roll ... 1 slice	30g	410	98
vanilla slice ... 1	135g	1155	276
Big Sister ... banana pecan/carrot ... nature cake	35g	625	149
vanilla/chocolate/orange ... low-fat cake	35g	424	101
Farmland ... pastries ... av all flavours ... 1		1060	253
Nanna's ... apple strudel ... ¼ strudel	100g	1060	253
sultana creme strudel ... ¼ strudel	100g	1470	351
Sara Lee ... bagels ... 1		943	225
banana cake ... ⅛ cake	45g	585	140
black forest ... ⅙ cake	83g	1020	244
cheesecake ... blueberry ... ⅙ cake	75g	840	201
peach mango ... ⅙ cake	75g	1013	242
chocolate Bavarian ... ⅛ cake	75g	1095	262
chocolate cake ... ⅛ cake	45g	650	155
Danish pastry ... apple ... 1 slice	100g	1370	327
blueberry ... 1 slice	100g	1060	253
continental ... 1 slice	100g	1354	324
pecan ... 1 piece	85g	1300	311
harlequin Bavarian ... ⅛ cake	75g	965	231
lemon Bavarian ... ⅙ cake	75g	934	223
mocca gâteau ... ⅛ cake	100g	1349	322
pound cake ... all-purpose ... ⅛ cake	40g	635	152
chocolate ... ⅛ cake	40g	620	148
sultana ... ⅛ cake	45g	697	167
Swiss cream celebration cake ... ¹⁄₁₀ cake	125g	1765	422

	MASS	KJ	CAL
calamari ... fried (Lebanese)	100g	1170	280
raw ... 1 tube	180g	590	141
sliced, floured, fried ... 1 cup	95g	725	173
camp pie ... canned	100g	710	170
cannelloni ... Leggo's ... dried ... 1 sv	33g	484	116
Findus Lean Cuisine ... with cheese ...1 sv	260g	1035	247
canola oil see oils			
cantaloupe/rockmelon see melon			
cape gooseberry	100g	200	48
capers ... 5	5g	5	1
cappuccino ... 1 cup	250ml	510	122
capsicum ... green ... boiled ... 1 cup chopped	110g	110	26
raw ... 1 cup chopped	120g	80	19
red ... boiled ... 1 cup chopped	145g	170	41
raw ... 1 cup chopped	120g	125	30
Edgell ... diced	100g	135	32
carambola ... flesh+skin+seeds ... 1 av	125g	290	69
caramels see confectionery			
caro ... coffee substitute ... 1 tsp	2.5g	40	10
carob bars see health-food bars			
carob drink powder see milk, flavoured			
carob flour ... 1 cup	100g	755	180
carob powder	100g	1555	372
carrot cake see cakes and pastries			
carrots ... baby ... boiled/raw ... peeled ... 1 av	16g	20	5
Birds Eye ... frozen	100g	165	39
Edgell ... canned	100g	115	27
Farmland/Golden Circle/McCain	100g	120	29
mature ... boiled ... peeled ... 1 cup	140g	155	37
canned	100g	135	32
raw ... peeled ... 1 med	81g	80	19
Birds Eye ... rings ... frozen	100g	165	39

	MASS	KJ	CAL
Edgell ... julienne ... canned	100g	150	36
cashew nuts ... roasted ... 15	30g	715	171
see also *snack foods*			
cassaba see *melon, honeydew*			
cassava ... boiled ... peeled ... ¼	145g	800	191
see also *tapioca*			
cassava bread	100g	1575	376
cassava flour	100g	1435	343
cauliflower ... boiled ... 1 stem + floweret	90g	70	17
canned	100g	100	24
frozen ... av all brands	100g	95	23
raw ... 1 stem + floweret	70g	55	13
Birds Eye ... in cheese sauce	100g	210	50
cauliflower cheese	100g	470	112
caviar ... lumpfish roe ... black ... 1 tbsp	19g	73	17
red ... 1 tbsp	19g	120	29
celeriac ... boiled ... peeled ... ½	115g	150	36
raw ... peeled ... ½	127g	150	36
celery ... boiled ... 1 cup chopped	125g	70	17
raw ... 1 stick	20g	10	2
cereals see *breakfast cereals*			

Cauliflower and Vegetable Soup

4 cups chicken stock
¼ large cauliflower
1 medium-sized potato
1 medium-sized carrot

1 stick celery
1 medium-sized onion
2 tablespoons dry sherry

Place stock in a large saucepan. Roughly chop the vegetables and add them to the chicken stock. Bring to the boil and then simmer for 30 minutes, or until vegetables are tender. Remove from heat and blend in a food processor until smooth. Return soup to saucepan, add the dry sherry and reheat. Serves 4 at 388 kJ (92 Cal) per portion.

	MASS	KJ	CAL
champagne	100ml	345	82
champignons ... Admiral ... in cream sauce	100g	418	100
Farmland ... whole ... no added salt	100g	100	24
chapati see **bread**			
chapati flour	100g	1410	337
chard see **silver beet**			
chats see **potatoes: new**			
cheese			
bel paese	30g	768	184
blue vein/cheshire/colby	30g	483	115
brie, Australian	30g	425	102
camembert ... av Australian/imported	30g	390	93
cheddar ... matured	30g	505	121
reduced-fat	30g	410	98
reduced-salt	30g	515	123
cottage ... creamed ... 2 tbsp	25g	130	31
low-fat ... 2 tbsp	25g	105	25
uncreamed ... 2 tbsp	25g	95	23
cotto	30g	265	63
cream cheese/jarlsberg	30g	433	103
Danish blue	30g	410	98
edam/pecorino	30g	448	107
fetta/neufchatel	30g	380	91

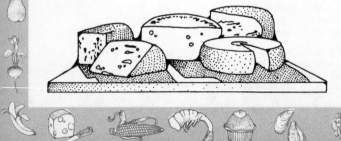

	MASS	KJ	CAL
low-salt	30g	470	112
reduced-fat	30g	290	69
fruited	30g	405	97
gloucester/havarti	30g	518	121
goat	30g	320	76
gorgonzola/romano	30g	470	112
gouda/raclette/roquefort/provolone	30g	463	111
gruyère	30g	520	124
mascarpone	30g	550	131
mozzarella/pizza	30g	400	95
reduced-fat	30g	360	86
parmesan	30g	535	128
processed ... cheddar ... canned	30g	420	100
sliced and packaged	30g	400	96
quark	30g	170	41
low-fat	30g	95	23
ricotta	30g	185	44
reduced-fat	30g	165	39
stilton	30g	575	137
Swiss	30g	475	114
Allowrie ... creamed cottage	30g	126	30
low-fat cottage	30g	108	26
Avalanche ... almond and curacao	30g	370	88
pepper log	30g	430	103
pineapple rum	30g	385	92
poppyseed fruit/smoky bacon	30g	410	98
Bega/Ibis ... cheddar ... mild/tasty/vintage	30g	511	122
so-lite ... reduced-fat	30g	440	105

Although high in kilojoules, parmesan cheese goes a long way because of its flavour, so substitute it for ordinary cheese as a topping for cooked meals.

	MASS	KJ	CAL
processed ... cheddar/super slices ... 1	30g	412	98
cheddar super-slims (slices) ... 1	30g	257	61
so-lite slices ... 1		312	74
Bodalla ... edam ... blocks/slices	30g	450	108
gouda ... blocks/slices	30g	465	111
tasty/mild/vintage cheddar	30g	504	120
reduced-fat and -salt cheddar	30g	436	104
Bulla ... cottage	30g	109	26
Chateau ... neufchatel	30g	380	91
Dairy Farmers ... low-fat, reduced-salt cottage	30g	115	27
natural creamed cottage...			
av all flavours	30g	130	31
Devondale ... trim n' tasty cheddar	30g	435	104
Gold'n Canola ... mild	30g	400	96
Jalna ... fetta ... 100% goat's milk	30g	227	54
skim milk cottage	30g	129	31
slicing cottage	30g	151	36
Kraft ... cheesestiks	20g	305	73
cracker barrel/mil-lel/Danish havarti	25g	420	100
Danish blue	25g	345	82
Danish camembert	25g	330	79
edam ... reduced-fat	25g	320	76
traditional	25g	345	82
gouda ... reduced-fat	25g	340	81
traditional	25g	400	96
light	25g	270	65
mozzarella ... traditional	25g	345	82
reduced-fat	25g	306	73
Philadelphia ... cream/soft cream	25g	355	85
light cream	25g	205	49
processed ... cheddar packets/loaf cans	20g	265	63

	MASS	KJ	CAL
deluxe cheddar slices ... 1 slice	21g	290	69
light singles ... 1 slice	21g	220	53
singles ... 1 slice	21g	250	60
romano ... traditional	25g	385	92
Swiss reduced-fat	25g	335	80
Lactos ... Cradle Valley edam	30g	420	100
Cradle Valley spring onion ... processed	30g	395	94
gouda	30g	470	112
Mersey Valley club	30g	490	117
neufchatel ... chocolate	30g	480	115
plain	30g	325	78
strawberry	30g	425	102
St Clair	30g	450	108
Tasmanian brie	30g	400	96
Tasmanian camembert	30g	440	105
with peppercorns	30g	385	92
Mainland ... av all flavours processed	30g	425	102
blue vein	30g	445	106
edam	30g	422	101
gouda	30g	460	110
light'n natural ... reduced-fat cheddar	30g	453	108
lite ones ... reduced-fat processed slices	30g	305	73
mild cheddar/tasty cheddar/vintage tasty	30g	520	124
mozzarella	30g	345	82
parmesan	30g	580	139
processed cheddar	30g	420	100
tasty colby	30g	495	118
Nimbin ... natural ... reduced-salt	30g	489	117
Norco ... cheddar ... reduced-fat	30g	420	100
mozzarella ... shredded	30g	377	90
ricotta	30g	140	33
Oak ... cheddar varieties	30g	535	128

	MASS	KJ	CAL
cottage	30g	175	42
cream	30g	430	103
Pauls ... continental-style low-fat	30g	117	28
cottage ... low-fat plain/peppercorn and herb	30g	103	25
natural/gherkin/garden salad	30g	125	30
Perfect Cheese ... grated parmesan	30g	574	137
light mozzarella	30g	323	77
pecorino/romano	30g	470	112
Renaissance ... edam ... reduced-fat	25g	320	76
gouda ... reduced-fat	25g	340	81
Swiss ... reduced-fat	25g	335	80
tasty	25g	420	100
Riviana ... blue vein	30g	460	110
brie	30g	420	100
camembert	30g	385	92
fruit ... av all flavours	30g	415	99
pepper roll	30g	425	102
swirl ... french onion/salmon	30g	437	104
Spring Grove ... reduced-fat and -salt	30g	408	98
Weight Watchers ... cottage	30g	115	27
individual slices ... 1 slice	21g	210	50
cheese souffle	100g	950	227
cheese spreads see *dips and spreads*			
cheesecake see *cakes and pastries*			
cherries ... glacé	100g	1420	339
raw ... 10 cherries	45g	85	20
stewed without sugar ... inc stone ... 20 cherries	100g	140	33
John West ... black in syrup	100g	266	64
SPC ... in syrup	100g	345	82
cherries, sour ... pitted	100g	319	76
chestnuts ... 4	20g	145	35
chewing gum see *confectionery*			

	MASS	KJ	CAL
chick pea spread see **dips and spreads:** homous			
chick peas ... boiled	100g	685	164
canned	100g	495	118
cooked (dahl)	100g	610	146
dry seed	100g	1315	314
chicken			
average cut ... roast ... meat + skin ... 1 sv	100g	1005	240
rotisseried ... lean+skin ... from ½ chicken	195g	1975	472
boneless, average ... baked ... lean + skin ... from ½ chicken	268g	2765	661
lean only ... from ½ chicken	213g	1665	398
skin only ... skin from ½ chicken	55g	1105	264
breast ... baked ... lean ... ½ breast	79g	520	124
lean + skin ... from ½ breast	97g	885	212
from whole baked chicken	100g	900	215
lean + skin + stuffing ... from whole rotisseried chicken	100g	900	215
crisp-skin (Chinese)	100g	860	206
drumstick ... baked ... lean + skin ... from whole baked chicken	48g	480	115
lean only ... from whole baked chicken	43g	375	90
leg qtr ... rotisseried ... lean + skin ... 1 av	99g	1120	268
liver ... floured, fried ... 1 sv	130g	1460	349
Griffs ... chicken mornay ... 1 sv	400g	1664	398
lemon chicken ... 1 sv	400g	2116	506
Singapore curry chicken ... 1 sv	400g	2508	599
Findus Lean Cuisine ... breast of chicken marsala ... 1 sv	230g	816	195
coconut chicken ... 1 sv	260g	1046	250

Avoid fatty meats when choosing cold meats for salads. Lean meats such as chicken, turkey and lean boiled ham should appear on your shopping list in place of salami and pâtés.

		MASS	KJ	CAL
	glazed chicken with vegetable rice ... 1 sv	240g	1087	260
Inghams				
	big dippers ... 1 sv	50g	720	172
	breast medallions ... honey and sesame ... 1 sv	100g	1037	248
	oriental lemon ... 1 sv	100g	988	236
	teriyaki ... 1 sv	100g	910	217
	breast patties ... 1 sv	85g	1010	241
	chipees ... spicy/tasty ... 1 sv	100g	1182	283
	crumbed fillets/breast tenders	100g	1045	250
	mini-drums ... edible portion	100g	1270	304
	nuggets ... 1/5 pkt	100g	1340	319
Plumrose ... deli ... canned		100g	590	141
chicken a la king		100g	800	191
chicken and almonds (Chinese)		100g	575	137
chicken and vegetable casserole ... 1 sv		200g	700	167
chicken basil (Thai)		100g	780	186
chicken cacciatore		100g	525	125
chicken chasseur... Healthy Choice ... 1 sv		310g	1050	250
chicken chop suey (Chinese)		100g	410	98
chicken chow mein (Chinese)		100g	705	168
chicken cordon bleu ... Baron's Table ... 1 sv		138g	1530	366
chicken croquettes ... deep-fried ... 1		55g	615	147
chicken curry ... Vesta ... 1 pkt made up ... 2 svs		218g	3397	812
chicken curry (Thai)		100g	570	136
chicken fricassee		100g	675	161
chicken ginger (Thai)		100g	770	184
chicken in peach sauce ... 1 sv		200g	1400	335
chicken kiev ... Baron's Table ... 1 sv		175g	1915	458
	Inghams ... 1 sv	100g	1170	280
chicken lemon (Chinese)		100g	820	196
chicken-liver pâté		100g	1285	307

	MASS	KJ	CAL
chicken provencal ... Mauri ... 1 sv	125g	220	53
chicken salad (Thai)	100g	495	118
chicken schnitzel ... Baron's Table ... 1 sv	150g	1615	386
chicken supreme ... Vesta ... 1 pkt made up ... 2 svs	236g	3884	928
chicken, tandoori... Healthy Choice ... 1 sv	270g	1213	289
chicken, take-away see *Hungry Jack's; Kentucky Fried Chicken; McDonald's*			
chicory ... boiled ... 1 cup chopped	145g	95	23
raw ... 1	48g	25	6
chiko roll ... deep-fried ... 1	165g	1560	373
chilli pickle	100g	1120	268
chilli sauce see *sauces, savoury*			
chillies ... banana ... boiled ... 1 av	55g	35	8
green ... boiled ... 1 av	20g	15	4
long, thin ... boiled ... 1 av	19g	20	5
red ... boiled ... 1 av	18g	25	6
raw ... 1 av	20g	25	6
Chinese broccoli ... raw	80g	120	29
Chinese cabbage see *cabbage*			
Chinese chard ... raw	75g	35	8
Chinese chives ... 1 tbsp chopped	4g	5	1
Chinese gooseberry see *kiwifruit*			
Chinese parsley ... raw	10g	13	3
Chinese salted fish ... steamed	100g	660	158
Chinese spinach see *spinach*			
Chinese zucchini ... raw	69g	60	14
chips see *potato chips*			
chives ... raw ... 1 tbsp chopped	4g	5	1
see also *spices, dried*			
chocolate biscuits see *biscuits*			
chocolate cake see *cakes and pastries*			
chocolate drink mix ... Jarrah ... all flavours ... 1 sv	12g	184	44
chocolate eclair see *cakes and pastries; confectionery*			

	MASS	KJ	CAL

chocolate see *confectionery*

chokoes ... boiled ... peeled ... 1 cup chopped ....140g.........115.........27

chop suey see *chicken chop suey; pork chop suey*

chops see *lamb; pork; veal*

chow mein see *chicken chow mein (Chinese)*

Christmas cake see *cakes and pastries*

Christmas pudding see *desserts and puddings*

chutney ... av all flavours ... 1 tsp ....5g..........45.........11

cider ... alcoholic ....100ml.......165.........39

                  Strongbow ... draught ....100ml.......185.........44

                                 dry...100ml.......155.........37

                                 sweet.......................................100ml.......215.........51

                                 white.......................................100ml.......227.........54

                  Woodpecker ....100ml.......180.........43

           non-alcoholic ... sweet ....100ml.......190.........45

clams ... canned ....100g........470.......112

      fresh ... without shells ....100g........410.........98

      Admiral ... baby ....100g........349.........83

clobaci see *luncheon meat*

coating mix see *seasoned coating mix*

Coca Cola see *drinks, carbonated*

cockles ... boiled ....100g........205.........49

cocktail frankfurts see *frankfurters*

cocktails ... bloody mary...100ml.......325.........78

          bourbon and soda.......................................100ml.......380.........91

          daiquiri...100ml.......775.......185

          gin and tonic..100ml.......320.........76

Alcohol is absorbed more quickly than other food nutrients. It is transported by the blood to the liver, where it is detoxified at the rate of $1/2$–1 standard drink per hour. Energy released from alcohol can ultimately be used by the body, but all excess energy is converted to fat.

	MASS	KJ	CAL
manhattan	100ml	940	225
martini	100ml	555	133
pina colada	100ml	780	186
screwdriver	100ml	345	82
tequila sunrise	100ml	460	110
tom collins	100ml	230	55
whisky sour	100ml	570	136
see also *spirits*			
cocoa powder ... 1 tbsp	77g	90	22
coconut ... dessicated ... ½ cup	45g	1120	268
fresh meat	100g	1525	364
shredded ... dry ... 1 cup	100g	843	201
coconut cream ... Admiral	100g	1480	354
coconut milk ... canned ... 1 tbsp	20g	165	39
drained from fresh nut	100g	90	22
cod ... baked	100g	710	170
dried, salted ... cooked	100g	585	140
raw	100g	545	130
fried in batter	100g	835	200
grilled	100g	400	96
poached	100g	395	94
inc bones + skin	100g	345	82
raw	100g	320	76
smoked ... simmered	100g	395	94
steamed	100g	350	84
inc bones + skin	100g	285	68
Baron's Table ... uncooked	100g	325	78
Frionor ... fillets ... uncooked	100g	294	70
cod liver oil see *oils*			
coffee ... black	250ml	25	6
black + 1 sugar	250ml	140	33
black + 1 sugar + cream	250ml	445	106

	MASS	KJ	CAL
black, decaffeinated, instant	250ml	25	6
dry ...instant ... 1 tsp	2.5g	10	2
iced + cream	250ml	445	106
iced + cream + ice-cream	250ml	645	154
white ... ¼ cup milk	250ml	195	47
2 tsp milk	250ml	55	13
30ml milk + 1 sugar	250ml	220	53
all milk ... reduced-fat	250ml	535	128
all milk ... whole	250ml	700	167
coffee mix... Jarrah ... av all flavours ... 1 sv	13g	236	56
combination chow mein (Chinese)	100g	625	149
confectionery			
butterscotch	100g	1760	421
caramels ... plain	100g	1710	409
plain + nuts	100g	1790	428
chewing gum	100g	1325	317
chocolate ... average ... 5–6 squares		610	146

	MASS	KJ	CAL
coated almond fudge	100g	1800	430
diabetic	100g	2305	551
nut milk	100g	2275	544
plain ... dark	100g	2235	534
milk	100g	2250	538
fondant ... chocolate	100g	1715	410
plain	100g	1525	364
fudge ... chocolate/vanilla	100g	1670	399
gumdrops/jelly beans/liquorice allsorts	100g	1465	350
licorice ... 20-cm strap	52g	500	120
lollypops	100g	1585	379
marshmallow ... chocolate	100g	1695	405
plain	100g	1350	323
muesli bars see **health-food bars**			
pastilles	100g	1065	255
peanut brittle	100g	1800	430
peppermint	100g	1635	391
sweets, boiled	100g	1370	327
toffee ... mixed	100g	1870	447
turkish delight ... no nuts	100g	1255	300
Allens ... anticol/barley sugar/soothers	100g	1490	356
bananas/E.S. mints/kool fruits/kool mints	100g	1622	388
fruit tingles	100g	1482	354
honey and eucalyptus/butterscotch	100g	1640	392
Irish moss	100g	1508	360
jelly beans	100g	1533	366
Cadbury			
bars ... cherry ripe ... 1	55g	1080	258
chomp ... av all flavours ... 1	30g	650	155
crunchie ... 1	50g	1070	256
flake ... 1	30g	2210	528
moro ... 1	70g	1360	325

	MASS	KJ	CAL
picnic ... 1	50g	1235	295
turkish delight ... 1	55g	915	219
caramello koala ... 1	20g	425	102
caramello rolls/peppermint rolls	55g	1125	269
chocolate blocks ... coconut rough	100g	2315	553
dairy milk	100g	2200	526
energy	100g	2155	515
fruit and nut	100g	2060	492
nut ... av all varieties	100g	2260	540
premium dark	100g	2140	511
snack	100g	1970	471
soft centres ... av all varieties	100g	1970	471
swiss chalet	100g	2155	515
top deck	100g	2270	543
white	100g	2285	546
freddo ... av all flavours ... 1	20g	425	102
white/milk ... 1	20g	275	66

	MASS	KJ	CAL
Fry's bars ... Fry's cream/five fruits ... 1	45g	830	198
garfield ... caramel ... 1	20g	410	98
chocolate ... 1	20g	450	108
honeycomb ... 1	15g	330	79
Green's ... fruit rainbow snacks	25g	467	112
Lifesavers ... all flavours	100g	1584	379
Mars ... Bounty bar	50g	1001	239
M & Ms ... milk	60g	1020	244
peanut	60g	1060	253
Maltesers	45g	918	219
Mars bar	60g	1100	263
Mars Almond bar	50g	1020	244
Milky Way ... choc whip	25g	460	110
milk whip	25g	468	112
Snickers bar	60g	1210	289
Twix bar	55g	1120	268
Nestlé chocolate ... Alpine Fruits	100g	2047	489
Club/Choc Bits/Plaistowe Cooking	100g	2190	523
Club Roasted Almond	100g	2100	502
Crunch	100g	2210	528
Dark Cooking/Choc Melts	100g	2240	535
Fruit 'n Nut/Easter Eggs	100g	2270	543
Full Cream Milk	100g	2240	535
Smarties	100g	1875	448
Pascal ... barley sugar/fruit bonbons/fruit drops	100g	1555	372
big strap/laces/rails	100g	1510	361
butterscotch	100g	1760	421
chews/choc/columbines/licorice	100g	1420	339
chocolate eclairs	100g	1885	451

If you brush your teeth straight after eating, the fresh taste in your mouth may help you to resist snacking.

	MASS	KJ	CAL
clinkers/country mints	100g	1910	457
jars ... barley sugar/bonbons/bulls eyes/humbugs	100g	1550	370
butterscotch/chocmint crunchies	100g	1660	397
jellies/jelly babies	100g	1315	314
jelly beans	100g	1535	367
jubes	100g	1405	336
licorice allsorts	100g	1585	379
marshmallows ... av all varieties	100g	1480	354
spearmint chews	100g	1395	333
twists ... chocolate	100g	1740	416
other varieties	100g	1510	361
Red Tulip ... after-dinner mints/thins	100g	1740	416
Cameo	100g	2030	485
choc-coated nuts	100g	2245	537
fruit jellies	100g	1350	323
liqueur cherries	100g	1940	464
sweethearts	100g	1905	455
Rowntree Hoadley ... bertie beetle	100g	2088	499
fantales/milk elegance	100g	1766	422
fruit gums	100g	1460	349
kit kat	100g	2090	500
milk aero	100g	2176	520
minties	100g	1405	336
smarties/dairy box	100g	1861	445
violet crumble	100g	1903	455
Stimorol ... bubble gum ... av all flavours ... 1		90	22
original /sportlife... sugarfree ... 1		14	3
Wander ... ovalteenies	15g	235	56
Wrigley ... chewing gum ... sugar-free tabs ... fruit	100g	1190	284
peppermint/ spearmint	100g	1125	269

	MASS	KJ	CAL
sugar pellets ... arrowmint/			
juicy fruit	100g	1277	305
PK	100g	1307	312
see also *health-food bars*			
cooking chocolate ... Cadbury	100g	2100	502
cooking compound ... Unicorp ... dark	100g	2260	540
copha ... 1 tbsp	20g	740	177
cordials ... average diluted (1:4) ... 1 glass	250ml	290	69
average undiluted ... 2 tbsp	40ml	225	54
Diet Cottees ... low-joule ... lemon ... 1 glass	250ml	20	5
lime/coola ... 1 glass	250ml	50	12
orange ... 1 glass	250ml	40	10
raspberry ... 1 glass	250ml	25	6
So Slim ... all flavours ... 1 glass	250ml	27	6
Weight Watchers ... low-joule citrus cup/razz berry/			
tropic punch ... 1 glass	250ml	33	8
corn see *sweetcorn*			
corn bread	100g	1575	376
corn chips see *snack foods*			
corn fritters ... Birds Eye	100g	917	219
corn meal	100g	1465	350
corn pasta ... Country Harvest ... gluten-free ... all types	100g	1520	363
corn syrup ... ⅓ cup		240	57
corned beef see *beef*			
cornflakes see *breakfast cereals*			
cornflour ... av all brands ... 1 tbsp	10g	145	35
cottage pie see *shepherds pie*			
courgettes see *zucchini*			
couscous ... cooked	100g	950	227
cow peas see *beans, blackeye*			
crab ... boiled	100g	535	128
canned ... in brine ... meat only ... 1 cup	190g	985	235

	MASS	KJ	CAL
steamed … meat only	100g	390	93
Admiral … crabmeat	100g	405	97
Green's … shredded crabmeat	100g	420	100
crab in black-bean sauce (Chinese)	100g	645	154
crackers see biscuits			
cranberries … raw	100g	195	47
cranberry sauce see sauces, sweet			
crayfish see lobster			
cream … aerosol	20g	245	59
fresh … 1 tbsp	20ml	305	73
pure (35% fat) … 1 tbsp	20g	280	67
reduced-fat … canned/fresh … 1 tbsp	20g	220	53
single … 1 tbsp	20ml	180	43
thickened … av all brands … 1 tbsp	20g	285	68
whipped … 1 tbsp	12g	174	42
Bulla … lite	20g	157	38
Pauls … 1 tbsp	20ml	350	84
thickened light … 1 tbsp	20ml	170	41
cream powder … Oak … full-cream powder	100g	2100	502
cream, sour … 35% fat … 1 tbsp	20ml	295	71
extra light … Pauls … 1 tbsp	20ml	158	38
light … Bulla … 1 tbsp	20ml	164	39
Calorie Counters … 1 tbsp	20ml	190	45
Dairy Farmers/Oak/Pauls … 1 tbsp	20ml	165	39
reduced-fat (18% fat) … 1 tbsp	20ml	190	45
Dairy Farmers … 1 tbsp	20ml	280	67
Jalna … reduced-fat … 1 tbsp	20ml	198	47
crème fraîche	100g	1840	440
crispbread see biscuits			
crisps see snack foods			
croissants … 1	65g	1070	256
Sara Lee … all-butter … 1	50g	670	160

	MASS	KJ	CAL
crumpets 1	55g	390	93
cucumber ... apple ... raw ... unpeeled ... 1	320g	95	23
common ... raw ... peeled ... 5 slices	40g	20	5
unpeeled ... 5 slices	45g	15	4
Lebanese ... raw ... unpeeled ... 1	97g	45	11
pickled ... 1 large	100g	40	10
Always Fresh ... original dill	100g	48	11
telegraph ... raw ... unpeeled ... 5 slices	45g	20	5
cucumber and yoghurt dip see *dips and spreads*			
cumquat see *kumquat*			
currants .... dried	100g	1145	274
curried prawns ... Griffs ... 1 sv	400g	1443	345
curried prawns and rice (Chinese)	100g	560	134
curry .... Heinz ... rice and beef ... supersnack	100g	480	115
custard .... baked with cereal	100g	720	172
banana	100g	450	108
with egg, baked/boiled	100g	455	109
Dairy Farmers	100g	430	103
Norco ... Nimbin low-fat	100g	300	72
Yomix ... vanilla ... added cream	100g	435	104
custard apple ... raw ... peeled ... flesh only ... 1/4	120g	365	87
custard mix ... Bingo ... egg	75g	1270	304
Foster Clark's ... egg	75g	1270	304

Slimmers' Tuna, Cucumber and Chives Dip

75 g peeled and chopped cucumber
100 g tuna in brine, drained and mashed
3 tablespoons buttermilk
2 level tablespoons low-fat natural yoghurt

1 teaspoon Worcestershire sauce
salt and pepper to taste
chopped chives

Blend cucumber and tuna until smooth. Add buttermilk, yoghurt, sauce and seasoning. Chill and sprinkle with chives before serving. Serves 1 at 288 kJ (69 Cal).

	MASS	KJ	CAL
quick	80g	1350	323
Green's ... instant ... 1 sachet	60g	1365	326
custard powder ... av all brands ... 1 tbsp	14g	200	48
cyclamate see *sugar substitutes*			
dahl see *chick peas; beans, mung; lentils*			
dairy dessert see *desserts and puddings*			
damson plums see *plums*			
dates ... dried ... pitted ... 1 av	7g	80	19
fresh ... raw ... inc stone	100g	600	143
raw ... diced	100g	1055	252
desserts and puddings			
apple crumble	100g	1145	274
blancmange	100g	460	110
bread-and-butter pudding	100g	670	160
chocolate mousse	100g	2165	517
Christmas pudding	100g	1325	317
golden syrup dumplings	100g	885	212
lemon delicious	100g	935	223
milk pudding	160g	880	210
pavlova ... + cream + strawberries	100g	1600	382
plum pudding ... canned	90g	875	209
rice pudding ... canned	100g	385	92

	MASS	KJ	CAL
sponge pudding ... jam-filled	100g	1280	306
steamed	100g	1395	333
steamed pudding ... chocolate	100g	1495	357
plain	100g	1395	333
trifle	100g	620	148
Divine Classics ... chocolate mousse	100g	712	170
dairy dessert ... creme caramel	100g	531	127
ETA ... blueberry meringue single-serve	100g	1515	362
lemon meringue single-serve	100g	1900	454
pine and coconut meringue single-serve	100g	1400	335
Farmland ... cheesecake ... original/strawberry	100g	1225	293
chocolate bavarian	100g	1360	325
Foster Clark's ... snak pack ... av all flavours	150g	815	195
Garden City ... dairy dessert ... all varieties	100g	220	53
Light Fruche ... av all flavours	100g	275	66
Oak ... dairy dessert	100g	590	141
low-cholesterol frozen dessert	100g	840	201
Pampas ... filo apple strudel	100g	1140	272
lovebites ... apple	100g	1350	323
berry	100g	1195	286
Robertson's ... Christmas pudding	100g	1295	310
Yogo see *yoghurt*			
Yoplait ... dairy dessert ... chocolate vigueur ... choc-caramel	100g	586	140
choc-malt	100g	601	144
chocolate	100g	610	146
grand miam/ petit miam ... av all flavours	100g	594	142
see also *custard*; *pies*, *sweet*			
dim sim ... deep-fried ... 1	50g	465	111
dips and spreads			
baba ghannouj (eggplant dip)	20g	200	48
cheddar spread	20g	245	59

	MASS	KJ	CAL
cheese wiz	20g	220	53
cream cheese dip ... flavoured ... 1 tbsp	22g	230	55
cream cheese spread	20g	285	68
Danish blue	20g	300	72
fish paste ... canned ... 1 tsp	5g	30	7
gorgonzola	20g	290	69
homous (chick pea spread)	20g	190	45
marmite/meat paste ... 1 tsp	5g	40	10
nutella (hazelnut spread)	20g	450	108
peanut butter	20g	530	127
skordalia (Greek)	20g	110	26
taramasalata	20g	200	48
tzatziki (cucumber and yoghurt dip)	20g	110	26
vegemite ... 1 tsp	5g	38	9
Dairy Farmers ... dips ... av all flavours ... 1 tbsp	20g	170	41
ETA ... peanut butter ... crunchy/smooth/traditional	20g	542	130
no added salt	20g	555	133
Farmland ... peanut butter ... crunchy/smooth ... no added salt	20g	535	128
Kraft ... barbeque dip/smoked oyster	20g	205	49
cheese spread	20g	260	62
cream cheese spread	20g	288	69
curried beef spread/devilled beef and ham ... 1 tsp	5g	42	10
curried salmon and prawn spread ... 1 tsp	5g	26	6
French onion dip/gherkin/onion and bacon style	20g	214	51
salmon, lobster and tomato spread ... 1 tsp	5g	25	6
salmon pastes ... av ... 1 tsp	5g	27	6
sandwich relish	20ml	125	30
spicy Mexican-flavour dip	20g	210	50
Lawrys ... 1 pack ... not made up ...			
avocado		200	48
bacon and onion/French onion		230	55
green onion		240	57

	MASS	KJ	CAL
seafood		190	45
Masterfoods ... lemon butter ... 1 tsp	10g	125	30
promite ... 1 tsp	5g	35	8
tomato ... chilli/mild/spicy	20g	36	9
Paul's ... cracka dips ... av all flavours	20g	155	37
Perfect Cheese ... smooth ricotta spread ... 1 tsp	10g	53	13
Peters Farm ... incredible spreadables ... av all flavours	20g	253	60
Philadelphia ... light dips ... av all flavours	20g	71	17
Sanitarium ... honey and glucose ... 1 tbsp	27g	355	85
dolmades see *vine leaves, stuffed*			
doughnuts ... cinnamon and sugar ... 1	50g	770	184
iced ... 1	80g	1425	341
Herbert Adams ... iced ring donuts	100g	1500	359
jam ball donuts	100g	1470	351
dressing see *salad dressing*			
drinking chocolate powder ... Cadbury ... 1 sv	10g	160	38
see also *chocolate drink mix*			
drinks, carbonated ... creamy soda	100ml	195	47
dry ginger ale	100ml	125	30
lemonade/lime	100ml	185	44
mineral water ... lemon	100ml	120	29
natural	100ml	0	0
sarsaparilla	100ml	195	47
soda water	100ml	0	0

Low-Joule Cheese, Garlic and Onion Dip

75 g onion, finely chopped
2 cloves garlic, crushed
3 tablespoons low-fat natural yoghurt

120 ml buttermilk
1 tablespoon grated parmesan cheese
chopped parsley

Mix together the onion and garlic and fold into yoghurt, buttermilk and cheese. Chill and sprinkle with parsley before serving. Serves 1 at 260 kJ (62 Cal).

	MASS	KJ	CAL
tonic water	100ml	150	36
Bisleri ... chinotto	100ml	175	42
lemon, lime and bitters	100ml	100	24
orange/lemon	100ml	117	28
Bulmer ... sparkling apple fruit-juice drink	100ml	155	37
Coca-Cola	100ml	171	41
Deep Spring Mineral Water ... lemon and lime	100ml	140	33
lemon, lime and orange	100ml	155	37
orange/orange and mango/ sparkling apple	100ml	170	41
orange and passionfruit	100ml	150	36
Devondale ... sparkling apple juice	100ml	155	37
Diet Coke	100ml	2	0
Diet Fanta	100ml	3	1
Diet Lift	100ml	7	2
Diet Sprite	100ml	4	1
Fanta ... orange	100ml	217	52
Kirks ... bitter lemon/lemon/lemonade	100ml	201	48
club lemon/sarsparilla	100ml	207	49
drinking dry ginger ale	100ml	186	44
orange soda squash	100ml	199	48
tonic water	100ml	145	35
Lift	100ml	180	43
Marchants ... club lemon soda squash/raspberry/lemonade	100ml	190	45
lime	100ml	200	48
pasito	100ml	195	47
pineapple/portello	100ml	170	41
Sprite ... lemonade	100ml	165	39
Sunraysia ... sparklers ... mandarin lime/orange	100ml	128	31
Tarax ... bitter lemon/wild raspberry	100ml	170	41
creamy soda/lemonade/tropical lime	100ml	180	43
low-joule lemonade	100ml	4	1

	MASS	KJ	CAL
orange drink/sunshine pine	100ml	190	45
drinks, sports... Cadbury Schweppes ... sportplus	100ml	120	29
Berri ... isosport edge ... all flavours	100ml	112	27
Isostar ... liquid ... 1 sv	250ml	291	70
powder ... 1 sv	40g + 500ml water	620	148
dripping see *lard*			
drop scones ... 2	50g	640	153
duck ... raw ... meat only	100g	515	123
roasted	100g	1310	313
dumplings ... plain	100g	885	212
dumplings, golden syrup see *desserts and puddings*			
eel ... fresh ... grilled/stewed	100g	840	201
raw	100g	700	167
smoked	100g	1380	330
egg ... boiled ... from 1 egg (55g)	48g	305	73
dried	100g	2455	587
fried ... from 1 egg (55g)	35g	375	90
poached ... from 1 egg (55g)	47g	295	71
raw ... from 1 egg (55g)	48g	285	68
scrambled ... 1 sv	110g	750	179
egg substitute	100g	680	163
egg white ... raw ... from 1 egg (55g)	31g	60	14
egg yolk ... raw ... from 1 egg (55g)	17g	225	54
eggnog see *milk, flavoured*			
eggplant ... baked	100g	260	62
boiled ... 1 cup sliced	195g	160	38

Scrambled eggs can be one of the most fattening ways to prepare eggs. Two with toast can amount to 1675 kJ (400 Cal). If you scramble 2 eggs with 2 tablespoons of skim milk in a non-stick pan and forgo butter on your toast the kilojoule content drops to 1090 kJ (260 Cal).

	MASS	KJ	CAL
eggplant dip see dips and spreads			
eggs, duck ... boiled	100g	820	196
eggs, turtle	100g	895	214
enchirito ... with cheese, beef and beans	100g	745	178
endive ... raw ... 1 cup chopped	55g	20	5
equal see sugar substitutes			
felafel	100g	990	237
fennel ... boiled/raw ... 1/2 bulb	165g	130	31
fenugreek leaves ... raw	100g	145	35
fettuccine carbonara ... McCain ... 1 sv	375g	2756	659
figs ... dried	100g	1130	270
glacé	100g	1250	299
raw ... 1 av	40g	70	17
fillet of lamb ... Healthy Choice ... 1 sv	310g	1048	250
fish ... baked ... 1 fillet	150g	450	108
battered, deep-fried ... 1 fillet	145g	1535	367
commercial ... battered, deep-fried ... 1 fillet	145g	1535	367
crumbed, fried ... 1 fillet	165g	1230	294
fried ... 1 fillet	104g	772	185
steamed/grilled ... 1 fillet	65g	260	62
Birds Eye ... hake steak ... garlic and herb ... 1 portion	100g	493	118
lemon and pepper ...1 portion	100g	454	109
natural ... 1 portion	100g	391	93

	MASS	KJ	CAL
light 'n healthy ... cheese crumbed ... 1 portion	63g	378	90
lightly crumbed ... 1 portion	63g	427	102
smoked cod steak ... 1 portion	100g	421	101
tempura batter ... 1 portion	71g	568	136
I & J ... extra light ... standard/lemon ... 1 fillet	62g	434	104
light and crispy ... crumb/seasoned ... 1 fillet	71g	674	161
golden batter ... 1 fillet	71g	793	190
lemon ... 1 fillet	71g	728	174
see also names of individual fish			
fish balls (Chinese) ... steamed	100g	220	53
fish cakes ... deep-fried	80g	920	220
frozen ... fried ... 1	70g	680	163
Birds Eye ... crumbed ... 3	100g	910	217
Thai	100g	695	166
fish cocktail ... battered, fried ... fish pieces ... 1	30g	350	84
fish curry	100g	1050	251
fish fingers ... frozen ... grilled ... 1	23g	215	51
Birds Eye ... frozen ... grilled ... 1	25g	199	48
I & J ... chunky	100g	807	193
standard	100g	857	205
tasty	100g	859	205
fish in cheese sauce ... I & J	100g	304	73
fish in lemon sauce ... I & J	100g	416	99
fish in parsley sauce ... I & J	100g	319	76
fish in white sauce	100g	605	145
fish spreads see *dips and spreads*			
fish stew	100g	520	124
fish sticks ... frozen ... pan-fried ... 1	22g	160	38
five-corner fruit see *carambola*			
flake ... battered, deep-fried ... 1 fillet	145g	1235	295

	MASS	KJ	CAL
crumbed, pan-fried ... 1 fillet	165g	1225	293
steamed	100g	525	125
flapjacks see *pancakes*			
flathead ... battered, deep-fried	100g	954	228
floured, pan-fried	100g	740	177
steamed	100g	485	116
flounder ... baked	100g	845	202
battered, fried	100g	1165	278
crumbed, fried	100g	950	227
grilled	100g	400	96
poached	100g	395	94
raw	100g	330	79
smoked	100g	505	121
inc bones + skin	100g	335	80
steamed	100g	350	84
inc bones + skin	100g	210	50
flour, arrowroot ... 1 tbsp	10g	156	37
flour, corn see *cornflour*			
flour, barley ... Lowan Whole Foods ... wholemeal	100g	1481	354
flour, gluten	30g	475	114
flour, maize see *cornflour*			
flour, millet	100g	1480	354
flour, potato	100g	2070	495
flour, rice	100g	1525	364
flour, rye ... Lowan Whole Foods ... wholemeal	100g	1398	334
flour, soya ... full-fat	100g	1755	419
low-fat	100g	1485	355
Lowan Whole Foods	100g	1760	421
flour, wheat ... fortified	100g	1525	364
plain ... white ... 1 cup	125g	1844	441
wholemeal ... 1 cup	135g	1579	378
self-raising ... white ... 1 cup	125g	1763	421

	MASS	KJ	CAL
wholemeal ... 1 cup	135g	1500	359
The Old Grain Mill ... self-raising ... wholemeal	100g	1457	348
White Wings ... av all types	100g	1485	355
foule moudamass (Lebanese)	100g	305	73
frankfurters ... battered, deep-fried ... 1	100g	1280	306
boiled ... 2	100g	1160	277
Plumrose ... canned	100g	717	171
French beans see *beans, green*			
French fries see *potato chips*			
fried rice ... Griffs ... 1 sv	350g	2017	482
fried rice (Chinese)	100g	930	222
frijoles ... with cheese	100g	566	135
fruit see individual fruits			
fruit bread see *bread*			
fruit cake see *cakes and pastries*			
fruit cocktail ... Golden Circle	100g	345	82
fruit cocktail ... SPC ... in syrup	100g	245	59
nutradiet ... artific. sweet	100g	120	29
fruit conserve see *jams and marmalades*			
fruit drinks ... Berri ... 35% apricot nectar	250ml	600	143
35% mango nectar	250ml	475	114
lemon squeeze	250ml	250	60
Custer and Williams ... orange crush	250ml	385	92
av all other flavours	250ml	458	109
Golden Circle ... av all flavours	250ml	450	108
Oak	250ml	425	102
Prima ... av all flavours	250ml	448	107
Sunburst ... av all flavours	250ml	453	108
Sunrise ... av all flavours	250ml	425	102
fruit juices			
grapefruit ... fresh	250ml	375	90
lemon/lime ... fresh	250ml	288	69

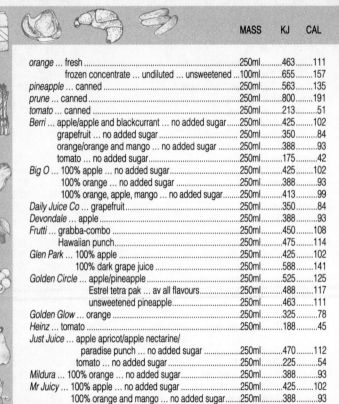

	MASS	KJ	CAL
orange ... fresh	250ml	463	111
frozen concentrate ... undiluted ... unsweetened	100ml	655	157
pineapple ... canned	250ml	563	135
prune ... canned	250ml	800	191
tomato ... canned	250ml	213	51
Berri ... apple/apple and blackcurrant ... no added sugar	250ml	425	102
grapefruit ... no added sugar	250ml	350	84
orange/orange and mango ... no added sugar	250ml	388	93
tomato ... no added sugar	250ml	175	42
Big O ... 100% apple ... no added sugar	250ml	425	102
100% orange ... no added sugar	250ml	388	93
100% orange, apple, mango ... no added sugar	250ml	413	99
Daily Juice Co ... grapefruit	250ml	350	84
Devondale ... apple	250ml	388	93
Frutti ... grabba-combo	250ml	450	108
Hawaiian punch	250ml	475	114
Glen Park ... 100% apple	250ml	425	102
100% dark grape juice	250ml	588	141
Golden Circle ... apple/pineapple	250ml	525	125
Estrel tetra pak ... av all flavours	250ml	488	117
unsweetened pineapple	250ml	463	111
Golden Glow ... orange	250ml	325	78
Heinz ... tomato	250ml	188	45
Just Juice ... apple apricot/apple nectarine/ paradise punch ... no added sugar	250ml	470	112
tomato ... no added sugar	250ml	225	54
Mildura ... 100% orange ... no added sugar	250ml	388	93
Mr Juicy ... 100% apple ... no added sugar	250ml	425	102
100% orange and mango ... no added sugar	250ml	388	93

Many fruit juices are relatively high in sugar and kilojoules. Diluting juices with mineral water or soda water cuts down on energy intake while making for a flavoursome, refreshing drink.

	MASS	KJ	CAL
Oak	250ml	425	102
Patra ... orange ... no added sugar	250ml	388	93
Popper ... apple	250ml	515	123
av all others	250ml	563	135
UHT ... av all flavours	250ml	450	108
Prima ... orange 100%	250ml	393	94
apple-blackcurrant	250ml	483	115
apple/orange-pine	250ml	438	105
apple-peach/tropical fruit	250ml	473	113
Pure'N Fresh ... apple ... no added sugar	250ml	425	102
orange ... no added sugar	250ml	388	93
Sanitarium ... apple ... reconstituted	250ml	450	108
grape ... dark shiraz/golden muscatel	250ml	825	197
med. dry red/white	250ml	700	167
sparkling red/white	250ml	750	179
orange/apple ... fresh	250ml	388	93
Schweppes ... orange	250ml	413	99
tomato	250ml	263	63
av all others	250ml	500	120

Tutti Frutti Dessert

1 level teaspoon powdered gelatine
1 tablespoon water
15 g slivered almonds
1 small carton low-fat natural yoghurt

25 g dried apricots, chopped
15 g glacé cherries, chopped
1 level tablespoon raisins
angelica to decorate

Sprinkle gelatine over the water in a small basin and leave to stand for 15 minutes. Stand basin in a pan of simmering water until the gelatine has dissolved. Heat almonds in a small non-stick saucepan, tossing until golden. Mix yoghurt with cooled gelatine mixture and stir in almonds and fruit. Spoon mixture into a mould. Chill until set. Turn dessert out onto a plate and decorate with angelica. Serves 1 at 1255 kJ (300 Cal).

	MASS	KJ	CAL
Spring Valley ... apple blends/pineapple/tropical ... av	250ml	463	111
nectars ... av	250ml	500	120
sparkling ... av	250ml	475	114
Sunburst ... apple/orange-mango ... no added sugar	250ml	500	120
orange	250ml	450	108
orange ... no added sugar	250ml	393	94
pineapple ... no added sugar	250ml	488	117
Sunpak ... orange, apple and mango/orange	250ml	375	90
sultana grape/dark grape	250ml	638	152
Sunraysia ... natural prune	250ml	628	150
natural raisin	250ml	898	215
red grape	250ml	613	147
Sunup ... 100% apple/ apple and blackcurrant ...			
no added sugar	250ml	425	102
100% grapefruit ... no added sugar	250ml	350	84
Valencio ... four fruits/wake up ... no added sugar	250ml	460	110
orange and mango/pineapple orange ...			
no added sugar	250ml	388	93
fruit mince ... Robertson's	100g	1150	275
fruit salad ... canned ... in heavy syrup ... 1 cup	270g	895	214
in pear juice ... 1 cup	255g	450	108
in syrup ... 1 cup	260g	530	127
fresh	100g	265	63
Golden Circle	100g	345	82
unsweetened	100g	185	44

	MASS	KJ	CAL
Goulburn Valley ... in fruit juice	100g	198	47
Weight Watchers ... handy pack	100g	116	28
fruit salad, tropical ... canned ... in heavy syrup ... 1 cup	270g	905	216
in pineapple juice ... 1 cup	260g	525	125

fudge see *confectionery*
galactobureko (Greek) see *cakes and pastries*
gammon see *ham*

garfish ... baked	100g	410	98
grilled	100g	400	96
poached	100g	395	94
raw	100g	320	76
smoked	100g	335	80
steamed	100g	350	84
garlic ... boiled ... peeled ... 2 cloves	5g	20	5
raw ... peeled ... 2 cloves	6g	25	6
White Wings ... granules	100g	920	220

garlic bread see *bread: sticks*

garlic prawns (Chinese)	100g	510	122
garlic prawns (Thai)	100g	820	196
gelatine powder	100g	1540	368
gemfish ... battered, deep-fried	100g	1195	286
crumbed, pan-fried	100g	1155	276
steamed	100g	940	225
ghee	100g	3695	883
Allowrie	100g	3700	884
gherkins	100g	75	18

gin see *spirits*

ginger ... boiled ... peeled ... 5 slices	10g	10	2
crystallised	100g	1425	341
ground	5g	55	13
raw ... peeled ... 1 tbsp grated	12g	15	4

gingerbread see *cakes and pastries*

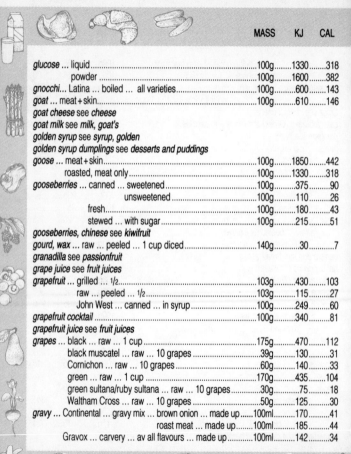

	MASS	KJ	CAL
glucose ... liquid	100g	1330	318
powder	100g	1600	382
gnocchi ... Latina ... boiled ... all varieties	100g	600	143
goat ... meat + skin	100g	610	146
goat cheese see *cheese*			
goat milk see *milk, goat's*			
golden syrup see *syrup, golden*			
golden syrup dumplings see *desserts and puddings*			
goose ... meat + skin	100g	1850	442
roasted, meat only	100g	1330	318
gooseberries ... canned ... sweetened	100g	375	90
unsweetened	100g	110	26
fresh	100g	180	43
stewed ... with sugar	100g	215	51
gooseberries, chinese see *kiwifruit*			
gourd, wax ... raw ... peeled ... 1 cup diced	140g	30	7
granadilla see *passionfruit*			
grape juice see *fruit juices*			
grapefruit ... grilled .. ½	103g	430	103
raw ... peeled ... ½	103g	115	27
John West ... canned ... in syrup	100g	249	60
grapefruit cocktail	100g	340	81
grapefruit juice see *fruit juices*			
grapes ... black ... raw ... 1 cup	175g	470	112
black muscatel ... raw ... 10 grapes	39g	130	31
Cornichon ... raw ... 10 grapes	60g	140	33
green ... raw ... 1 cup	170g	435	104
green sultana/ruby sultana ... raw ... 10 grapes	30g	75	18
Waltham Cross ... raw ... 10 grapes	50g	125	30
gravy ... Continental ... gravy mix ... brown onion ... made up	100ml	170	41
roast meat ... made up	100ml	185	44
Gravox ... carvery ... av all flavours ... made up	100ml	142	34

	MASS	KJ	CAL
gravy maker/supreme ... made up	100ml	110	26
gravyboat ... instant gravy mix ...			
av all flavours ...made up	100ml	130	31
supreme chicken ... made up	100ml	120	29
supreme low-joule ... made up	100ml	70	17
supreme salt-reduced ... made up	100ml	115	27
Maggi ... rich gravy ... made up	100ml	120	29
White Wings ... brown gravy mix ... made up	100ml	160	38
gravy mix ... made up	100ml	75	18
light and golden gravy mix ... made up	100ml	145	35
Greek foods see names of individual foods			
green pepper see *capsicum*			
greengage plums see *plums*			
grissini sticks see *bread: sticks*			
grouse ... roasted ... boneless	100g	730	174
guavas ... canned in syrup	100g	255	61
raw ... flesh + skin seeds ... 1 av	113g	115	27
guinea fowl ... raw	100g	665	159
gurnard, long finned ... baked	100g	410	98
grilled	100g	400	96
poached	100g	395	94
raw	100g	320	76
smoked	100g	335	80
steamed	100g	350	84
haddock ... fried	100g	690	165
raw	100g	320	76
smoked	100g	430	103
steamed	100g	415	99
steamed ... inc bones + skin	100g	315	75
Frionor ... fillets	100g	350	84
haggis ... boiled	100g	1290	308

	MASS	KJ	CAL
hake ... raw	100g	350	84
halibut, tropical ... baked	100g	410	98
grilled	100g	400	96
poached	100g	395	94
raw	100g	320	76
smoked	100g	335	80
steamed	100g	350	84
halva	100g	2570	614
ham ... leg ... canned ... av all brands	100g	470	112
lean ... 1 slice	25g	105	25
lean and fat ... canned ... 2 slices	35g	165	39
non-canned ... 1 slice	25g	145	35
with fat ... cured ... boned ... pressed slices	100g	455	109
on the bone ... cooked ... slices without bone	100g	950	227
prosciutto	100g	1445	345
shoulder ... canned ... av commercial brands	100g	495	118
cured ... boned, pressed slices	100g	465	111
lean ... non-canned ... 1 slice	25g	115	27
lean+fat ... canned ... 2 slices	35g	175	42
unspecified cut ... lean+fat ... 1 slice	25g	130	31
non-canned ... 2 slices	35g	170	41
Plumrose ... canned ... deli	100g	590	141
leg	100g	445	106
ham and cheese submarine ... with potato crisps ... 1 sv	215g	2625	627
Pizza Hut	100g	1240	296
ham sandwich see *sandwiches*			
ham steak ... grilled	100g	680	163
raw	100g	520	124
hamburger mince ... simmered, drained ... 1 cup	170g	1535	367
hamburger patties ... crumbed ... frozen ... fried ... av all brands	100g	1420	339
frozen ... fried ... av all brands	100g	1205	288
grilled ... av all brands	100g	1100	263

	MASS	KJ	CAL
Birds Eye	100g	1090	261
Farmland	50g	630	151
hamburgers ... plain ... 1	170g	1590	380
with bacon ... 1	185g	1955	467
with cheese ... 1	195g	2110	504
with onions ... 1	100g	1095	262
hazelnut spread see *dips and spreads*			
hazelnuts ... shelled	100g	2680	641
health-food bars			
Europe ... apricot and coconut ... 1	55g	775	185
cherry coconut ... 1	45g	830	198
fruit and nut roll ... 1	45g	975	233
fruit nougat ... 1	45g	780	186
ginger ... 1	40g	715	171
honey log ... 1	45g	1025	245
sesame ... 1	45g	865	207
summer roll ... 1	45g	1010	241
tropical fruit ... 1	45g	665	159
Gold Crest ... flips ... choc-coated honeycomb banana ... 1 bar	31g	615	147
peach raspberry/strawberry banana ... 1 bar	31g	515	123
white-choc-coated apricot passionfruit ... 1 bar	31g	665	159
fruitz ... choc-coated cherry coconut ... 1 bar	31g	597	143
yoghurt-coated apricot passionfruit ... 1 bar	31g	566	135
yoghurt-coated fruit salad ... 1 bar	31g	605	145
Uncle Toby's ... muesli bars ... choc chip ... 1 bar	31g	551	132

Aim to get 50–60 per cent of your daily kilojoules from cereals and complex carbohydrates (pasta, rice, bread, breakfast cereals and potatoes).

	MASS	KJ	CAL
fruit tops ... 1 bar	33g	575	137
three fruits/tropical fruits ... 1 bar	31g	500	120
yoghurt top ... 1 bar	31g	578	138

Healthy Choice see names of individual meals
heart see *beef; lamb*
herbs see *spices, dried*

	MASS	KJ	CAL
herrings ... canned	100g	840	201
in tomato sauce	100g	740	177
fried	100g	975	233
inc bones	100g	860	206
grilled	100g	830	198
inc bones	100g	560	134
kippered	100g	905	216
pickled	100g	930	222
raw	100g	970	232
Admiral ... herring fillets ... assorted	100g	715	171
John West ... in tomato sauce	100g	804	192
King Oscar ... fillets in tomato sauce	100g	860	206
herrings, Atlantic ... raw	100g	735	176
herrings, Pacific ... raw	100g	410	98

homous see *dips and spreads*

	MASS	KJ	CAL
honey ... av all brands ... 1 tbsp	27g	365	87

honeydew melon see *melon*

	MASS	KJ	CAL
horseradish	100g	250	60
horseradish cream ... Masterfoods	5g	30	7

hot cross buns see *buns*

	MASS	KJ	CAL
hot dog ... roll + frankfurt + sauce ... 1 av		1290	307

Plan before you start your diet. Understand the strengths and weaknesses in your eating habits and take them into account. Try to build into your shopping list low-fat, low-sugar and high-fibre alternatives to your staple foods.

	MASS	KJ	CAL
hundreds and thousands ... 1 tbsp	5ml	65	15
Hungry Jack's ... Apple Pie ... 1	1005	240	
Bacon Double Cheeseburger ... 1	2065	494	
Bacon Double Cheeseburger Deluxe ... 1	2376	568	
Cheese Burger ... 1	1298	310	
Chicken Nuggets ... 1	246	59	
French Fries ... small	950	227	
regular	1414	338	
large	1774	424	
Great Aussie Burger ... 1	2476	592	
Grilled Chicken Burger ... 1	1695	405	
Mini Burger ... 1	1113	266	
Ocean Catch Sandwich ... 1	1609	385	
Onion Rings ... regular	1875	448	
large	2500	598	
Sauces (for nuggets) ... per portion	101	24	
Sundae ... caramel ... 1	1028	246	
chocolate ... 1	1008	241	
strawberry ... 1	913	218	
Thickshake ... av all flavours ... 1	1170	280	
Whopper ... 1	2517	602	
Whopper Junior ... 1	1424	340	
Whopper Junior with Cheese ... 1	1609	385	
Whopper with Bacon/Cheese ... 1	2890	691	
Whopper with Egg ... 1	2642	631	
Yumbo ... 1	1395	333	
ice-block mix powder	100g	1240	296

ice-cream /ice confections

	MASS	KJ	CAL
vanilla ice-cream ... commercial ... av all brands ... 1 scoop	45g	375	90
vanilla ice confection ... commercial ... av all brands ... 1 scoop	45g	330	79
Bulla ... lite'n natural low-fat	100g	431	103

	MASS	KJ	CAL
frozen fruit'n yoghurt	100g	568	136
soft-serve	100g	817	195
Baskin Robbins ... plain ... 1 sv	90g	1110	265
Buttercup ... vanilla ... 1 sv	50g	400	96
Cadbury ... cherry ripe	60ml	650	155
crunchie	70ml	860	206
tempo	95ml	820	196
Dairy Bell ... frusen glädjè ... dietary dairy dessert	100g	444	106
lite ... polyunsaturated, no added sugar	100ml	234	56
vanilla ... reduced-fat ... ice confection	100ml	320	76
Everest Colonial ... gelato ... milk-based	100g	700	167
water-based	100g	380	91
tofu dessert ... av all flavours	100g	559	134
vanilla bean ice-cream ... low-fat	100g	600	143
Fruche ... soft-frozen	100g	263	63
Jalna ... soft-serve	100g	535	128
Nice-n-Lite ... 1 sv	50g	250	60
Norco ... natural fruit ice	67g	229	55
Oak	100g	840	201
Pauls ... extra cream ... double choc chip ... 1 scoop	100ml	435	104
peppermint ... 1 scoop	100ml	428	102
vanilla ... 1 scoop	100ml	380	91
hava-heart ... 1	77g	935	223
standard ... choc/neopolitan/van. ... 1 scoop	100ml	379	91
Peters ... alfresko ... 1	95g	597	143
billabong ... barney banana/choc natural ... 1	82g	448	107
bubbleberry ... 1	82g	629	150
choc mint/triple swirl	89g	487	116
carbo-modified	100ml	430	103
choc wedge ... av all flavours ... 1	70g	843	201
choc-o-malt ... 1	130g	675	161
drumstick ... mac nut caramel ... 1	79g	963	230

	MASS	KJ	CAL
mint chip ... 1	77g	823	197
triple choc ... 1	82g	897	214
eskimo pie ... vanilla ... 1	87g	1192	285
frisco	72g	834	199
frosty fruits ... 1	79g	314	75
frozen yoghurt ... av all flavours ... 1	93g	535	128
fruit de light ... 1	63g	219	52
heaven on a stick ... almond ... 1	99g	1106	263
choc/vanilla ... 1	97g	1081	258
icy pole ... raspberry/lemonade/ice graffiti ... 1	77g	209	50
light and creamy ... choc/strawb swirl ... 1 scoop	100ml	306	73
vanilla ... 1 scoop	100ml	290	69
light and creamy exotics ... classic strawb/peach passion ... 1 scoop	100ml	308	74
butterscotch crunch ... 1 scoop	100ml	356	85
monaco bar ... 1	73g	917	219
microfreeze thickshake ... 1 ... av all flavours		1293	309
natural ... choc caramel eclair/golden crunch ... 1 scoop	100ml	518	124
rich vanilla/wildberrry swirl ... 1 scoop	100ml	435	104
oasis ... av all flavours ... 1	77g	297	71
split ... pine lime/raspberry ... 1	63g	318	76
twister ... av all flavours	89g	725	173
vitari ... av all flavours ... 1 scoop	100ml	246	59

	MASS	KJ	CAL
weight watchers ... 1 scoop	100ml	281	67
Sara Lee ... Classic ... French vanilla	100ml	1076	257
peach mango	100ml	863	206
strawberries and cream	100ml	897	214
ultra chocolate	100ml	1035	247
Classic Light... cappuccino swirl	100ml	770	184
French vanilla	100ml	725	173
strawberries and berry	100ml	715	171
Snow Boy ... polyunsat. van. ice/no-milk van. honey ...			
3 scoops	150ml	570	136
Streets ... blue ribbon hearts ... 1		795	190
boomy ... 1		199	47
cal control slices	100ml	247	59
calippo ... lemon ... 1		475	114
orange ... 1		318	76
choc block ... vanilla ... 1		901	215
cornetto ... choc mint/chocolate ... 1		949	227
strawberry/wild strawberry ... 1		859	205
vanilla ... 1		866	207
finger ... 1		258	62
fresh yoghurt strawberry ... 1		496	119
fruiti yo ... 1		377	90
ice-cream slices	100ml	416	99
log ... viennetta cappuccino	100ml	574	137
magnum ... dark ... 1		1585	379
oz block ... cola/lemonade ... 1		216	52
paddle pops ... banana/rainbow ... 1		511	122
blue bubblegum/strawberrychoc ... 1		556	133
splice ... pine lime ... 1		379	91
triple treat ... 1		1018	243
tubs ... blue ribbon ... chocolate/vanilla	100ml	386	92
light strawberry	100ml	393	94

	MASS	KJ	CAL
toffee cream	100ml	463	111
vanilla light	100ml	350	84
Homer Hudson ... butter pecan/chocolate			
rock	100ml	1126	269
hoboken crunch	100ml	1048	250
super saver ... vanilla/neapolitan	100ml	398	95
yoghurt fruit salad ... 1		439	105
yoghurt strawberry ... 1		467	112
Taranto's ... gelato classico ... milk-based	100ml	300	72
water-based	100ml	200	48
premium natural ice-cream	100ml	380	91
tofu glace	100ml	295	71
Weight Watchers ... chocolate/vanilla ... 1 sv	100ml	285	68
ice-cream cones ... unfilled ... 1 small	5g	80	19
ice-cream mix ... Pauls ... UHT soft-serve mix	100g	540	129
icing ... almond see *marzipan*			
chocolate	100g	1460	349
fondant	100g	1605	384
marshmallow	100g	1264	302
warm	100g	1405	336
icing sugar ... pure/soft	100g	1635	391
Green's ... chocolate icing mix	100g	1580	378
plain icing mix	100g	1755	419
Indian chicken biryani ... Continental Easy Meals ... per pack		636	152

	MASS	KJ	CAL
Indonesian beef stir-fry ... Continental Easy Meals ... per pack		718	172
Irish stew ... canned ... av commercial brands	100g	360	86
home-made	100g	520	124
Farmland	100g	515	123
Harvest	100g	260	62
jackfruit ... raw ... peeled ... flesh only ... 1/4	201g	650	155
jams and marmalades ... jam ... all flavours ... av ... 1 tsp	10g	110	26
marmalade ... all flavours ... av ... 1 tsp.	10g	110	26
Country Harvest ... av all flavours ... 1 tsp	10g	50	12
IXL ... apricot jam ... 1 tsp	10g	119	28
av all other flavours ... 1 tsp	10g	110	26
Monbulk ... av all flavours ... 1 tsp	10g	115	27
Pureharvest ... spreadable fruit ... all flavours ... 1 tsp	10g	100	24
Quality Foods ... av all flavours ... 1 tsp	10g	65	16
Robertson's ... av all flavours ... 1 tsp	10g	106	25
Weight Watchers ... av all flavours ... 1 tsp	10g	11	3
jelly ... low-joule ... made up ... 1 sv	100g	15	4
made with milk ... made up ... 1 sv	100g	365	87
made with water ... made up ... 1 sv	100g	250	60
Aero Jelly-Lite Low-joule/Diet Cottees ... made up ... 1 sv.	100g	30	7
Aero Premium/Aeroplane ... made up ... 1 sv	100g	265	63
Country Harvest ... all flavours ... made up ... 1 sv	100g	385	92
So Slim ... made up ... 1 sv	100g	36	9
Pioneer ... low-joule ... strawberry ... made up ... 1 sv	100g	30	7
jelly beans see *confectionery*			
jelly crystals	100g	1235	294
Country Harvest ... low-protein ... all flavours	100g	1570	374
John Dory ... fried	100g	905	215

	MASS	KJ	CAL
steamed	100g	385	92
junket ... 1sv	100g	330	79
kafta (Lebanese)	100g	910	217
kale ... boiled	100g	160	38
raw	100g	180	43
kangaroo meat	100g	625	149
kedgeree	100g	635	151
Kentucky Fried Chicken ... bacon and cheese chicken fillet burger ... 1	193g	2063	493
bean salad ... 1 sv	110g	622	149
chicken fillet burger ... 1	170g	1785	427
coleslaw ... 1 sv	110g	440	105
Colonel Burger ... 1	114g	1197	286
Kentucky nuggets ... 1	18g	166	40
mashed potato and gravy ... 1 sv	110g	564	135
original recipe chicken ... av piece	69g	897	214
potato salad ... 1 sv	110g	615	147
works burger ... 1	233g	2179	521
kibbi (Lebanese) ... fried	100g	910	217
vegetarian ... baked	100g	1075	256
kibbi nayeh (Lebanese)	100g	710	169
kidney see *beef; lamb*			
kippers ... baked	100g	855	204
Admiral ... fillets	100g	938	224
snacks	100g	777	186
kiwifruit ... flesh + seeds ... 1 fruit	78g	160	38
kohlrabi ... boiled ... peeled ... 1 cup sliced	175g	265	63
raw ... peeled ... 1 cup sliced	150g	205	49

Check nutritional information accompanying food you buy. Avoid any food containing more than 3 grams of fat per 420 kJ (100 Cal).

	MASS	KJ	CAL
kumara see *sweet potato*			
kumiss	100g	1615	385
kumquat ... canned	100g	575	137
raw ... 1 small	7g	10	2
lady fingers (Lebanese)	100g	1195	285
lady fingers vegetarian (Lebanese)	100g	1365	325
lamb			
boneless ... average cut			
cooked ... lean ... 1 cup diced	190g	1455	348
lean+fat ... 1 cup diced	182g	1805	431
brains ... crumbed, fried	100g	1220	292
simmered ... 1 set	80g	450	108
breast ... boneless ... rolled ... baked	100g	1210	289
rolled, stuffed, baked ... 1 boneless slice	60g	725	173
chump chop ... grilled ... lean ... 1 av	56g	475	114
lean+fat ... 1 av	65g	770	184
cutlets ... crumbed, fried ... lean	100g	1435	343
lean+fat	100g	1945	465
heart ... baked ... 1 av	70g	540	129
kidney ... fried	100g	890	213
simmered ... 1 cup sliced	150g	915	219
leg ... baked ... lean ... 1 boneless slice	41g	305	73
lean+fat ... 1 boneless slice	45g	420	100
liver ... fried ... 1 slice	40g	405	97
mid-loin chop ... grilled ... lean ... 1 av	34g	250	60
lean+fat ... 1 av	48g	735	176
mince ... cooked	100g	1265	302
neck chop ... simmered ... lean ... 1 av	40g	425	102
lean+fat ... 1 av	50g	740	177
rib-loin cutlet ... grilled ... lean ... 1 av	29g	235	56
lean+fat ... 1 av	39g	555	133

	MASS	KJ	CAL
shank ... simmered ... lean ... 1 av	87g	655	157
lean+fat ... 1 av	99g	925	221
shoulder ... baked ... lean ... 1 boneless slice	22g	170	41
lean+fat ... 1 boneless slice	30g	360	86
tongue ... canned ... av all brands ... 5 slices	100g	810	194
simmered ... 1 av	55g	635	152
lamb casserole ... with vegetables	100g	585	140
without vegetables	100g	615	147
lamb Italian ... Healthy Choice ... 1 sv	250g	950	227
lamb's fry and bacon ... fried	100g	1840	440
Lancashire hotpot	100g	480	115
lard/dripping	20g	755	180
lasagne ... fresh-baked	100g	725	173
frozen ... av all brands	100g	530	127
Healthy Choice ... 1 sv	290g	1015	243
Tandaco ... one-pan dinner ... $^1/_4$ pkt	50g	665	159
lasagna, tuna see *tuna lasagna*			
lasagna, zucchini see *zucchini lasagna*			
lassi	100g	1575	376
Lean Cuisine see names of individual meals			
leatherjacket ... fried	100g	730	174
raw	100g	310	74
steamed	100g	415	99
Lebanese bread see *bread: flat breads*			
Lebanese foods see names of individual foods			

	MASS	KJ	CAL
lecithin ... The Old Grain Mill ... 98% unbleached granules ... 1 tbsp		210	50
leeks ... boiled ... 1 cup sliced	165g	165	39
raw ... 1 av	83g	90	22
lemon butter/curd	100g	1215	290
lemon ginger sauce with vegetables ... Kan Tong	100g	295	71
lemon juice ... fresh	100ml	110	26
lemon meringue see *pies, sweet*			
lemonade see *drinks, carbonated*			
lemons ... raw ... peeled ... flesh only ... 1 lemon	99g	95	23
lentils ... boiled (dahl) ... 1/2 cup	100g	295	71
dried ... 1/2 cup	100g	1405	336
Sanitarium ... savoury brown ... 1/4 can	110g	286	68
lettuce ... butter .... raw ... 3 leaves	100g	60	14
common ... raw ... 1 leaf	50g	15	4
cos ... raw ... 1 cup shredded	65g	45	11
iceberg ... raw	100g	55	13
mignonette ... raw ... 1 cup pieces	45g	25	6
radicchio ... raw	50g	15	4
lime juice ... fresh	100ml	115	27
limes ... raw .. peeled ... flesh only ... 1	49g	45	11
ling ... raw	100g	370	88
linseed ... ground ... Healtheries	100g	2295	549
liqueurs ... apricot/peach brandy/kirsch	20ml	135	32
benedictine/chartreuse/galliano/ouzo/sambuca	20ml	335	80
cherry brandy	20ml	215	51
cointreau/van der hum/grand marnier/advocaat	20ml	235	56
creme de menthe/malibu/tia maria/baileys/			
drambuie/kahlya	20ml	250	60
curacao	20ml	260	62
liver see *beef*; *chicken*; *veal*			
liver paste see *liverwurst*			
liver pâté see *pâté*			

	MASS	KJ	CAL
liverwurst	100g	1420	339
calf	100g	1285	307
chicken	100g	1300	311
lobster ... boiled ... meat only ... 1 cup	165g	670	160
canned	100g	400	96
raw	100g	370	88
lobster mayonnaise	100g	1100	263
lobster paste	100g	755	180
lobster thermidor ... 1 in shell	400g	1700	406
lobster with ginger and shallots (Chinese)	100g	560	134
locusts	100g	565	135
loganberries ... canned ... sweetened	100g	295	71
raw ... 1 av	13g	15	4
loquats ... canned	100g	350	84
lotus tubers ... canned	100g	65	16
lucozade	100ml	300	72
luffa, angled ... raw ... peeled ... 1 cup diced	135g	70	17
luncheon meat ... beef German/ham and chicken roll	100g	970	232
Berliner fleischwurst	100g	945	226
cabanossi	100g	1525	364
chicken roll	100g	630	151
Devon/chicken Devon/ham and chicken	100g	980	234
fritz	100g	1015	243
garlic roll	100g	1030	246
ham sausage	100g	1140	272
liverwurst	100g	1155	276
luncheon roll	100g	1225	293
mortadella/clobaci	100g	1355	324
Polish	100g	1005	240
polony	100g	1170	280
salami ... av all varieties	100g	1785	427
Strasbourg	100g	1025	245

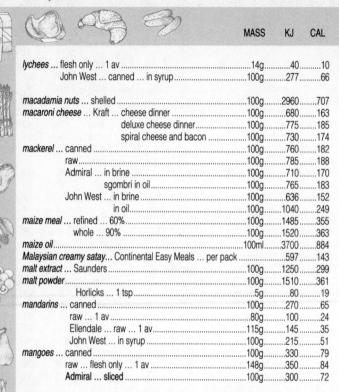

	MASS	KJ	CAL
lychees ... flesh only ... 1 av	14g	40	10
John West ... canned ... in syrup	100g	277	66
macadamia nuts ... shelled	100g	2960	707
macaroni cheese ... Kraft ... cheese dinner	100g	680	163
deluxe cheese dinner	100g	775	185
spiral cheese and bacon	100g	730	174
mackerel ... canned	100g	760	182
raw	100g	785	188
Admiral ... in brine	100g	710	170
sgombri in oil	100g	765	183
John West ... in brine	100g	636	152
in oil	100g	1040	249
maize meal ... refined ... 60%	100g	1485	355
whole ... 90%	100g	1520	363
maize oil	100ml	3700	884
Malaysian creamy satay ... Continental Easy Meals ... per pack		597	143
malt extract ... Saunders	100g	1250	299
malt powder	100g	1510	361
Horlicks ... 1 tsp	5g	80	19
mandarins ... canned	100g	270	65
raw ... 1 av	80g	100	24
Ellendale ... raw ... 1 av	115g	145	35
John West ... in syrup	100g	215	51
mangoes ... canned	100g	330	79
raw ... flesh only ... 1 av	148g	350	84
Admiral ... sliced	100g	300	72

*T*he season of mango madness is one of many dangers. Who knows what crazy idea a Commissar might come up with while under the influence of the dreaded mango fruit.

Northern Territory News, 22 September 1984

	MASS	KJ	CAL

maple syrup see *sauces, sweet*
margarine, cooking ....100g 3015 721
           Tulip ....100g 3000 717
margarine, table ... av all brands ... 1 tbsp ....15g 455 109
        Devondale ... dairy extra soft ... 1 tbsp ....15g 285 68
        ERA ... Flora Light ... polyunsaturated
          spread ... 1 tbsp ....15g 277 66
                margarine spread ... 1 tbsp ....15g 356 85
        Gold'n Canola ... mono-unsaturated ...
          lifestyle reduced-fat spread ... 1 tbsp .....15g 330 79
        Meadow Lea ... polyunsaturated ... 1 tbsp ....15g 450 108
marinade mix see *sauces, savoury*
marmalade see *jams and marmalades*
marmite see *dips and spreads*
marrow, vegetable ... boiled ... peeled ... 1 cup diced ....220g 175 42
        raw ... peeled ... 1 cup diced ....135g 95 23
martini see *cocktails*
marzipan ....30g 555 133
mayonnaise ... Country Harvest ... soya ... 1 tbsp ....20ml 615 147
        Gold'n Canola ... 1 tbsp ....20ml 307 73
        Hain light canola ... 1 tbsp ....20ml 358 86
        Heinz ... 1 tbsp ....20ml 300 72
        Kraft ... cholesterol-free ... 1 tbsp ....20ml 142 34
              light ... 1 tbsp ....20ml 209 50
              polyunsaturated ... 1 tbsp ....20ml 280 67
        Nature's Garden ... 1 tbsp ....20ml 640 153
        Praise ... light ... 1 tbsp ....20ml 204 49
              no-cholesterol ... 1 tbsp ....20ml 303 72

Weigh yourself regularly, say once a week in the morning. Don't hop on and off the scales every day as weight fluctuation, which can be the product of many different factors, could be discouraging.

	MASS	KJ	CAL
Weight Watchers	20ml	146	35
McDonald's ... apple pie ... 1	87g	1148	274
big mac ... 1	215g	2102	502
cheeseburger ... 1	117g	1351	323
chef salad ... 1	268g	905	216
chicken mcnuggets ... 1	19g	226	54
chocolate milk shake ... 1	304ml	1411	337
cookies ... 1 box	60g	1216	291
English muffin ... 1	68g	805	192
filet-o-fish ... 1	152g	1605	383
French fries ... large carton	169g	1788	427
regular carton	81g	857	205
garden salad	213g	470	112
hashbrown ... 1	58g	758	181
hot fudge sundae ... 1	163g	1113	266
junior burger ... 1	103g	1169	279
mcfeast ... 1	238g	2237	535
mild curry sauce ... per portion	32g	184	44
quarterpounder and cheese ... 1	205g	2499	597
sausage mcmuffin ... 1	116g	1413	338
sausage mcmuffin with egg ... 1	164g	1771	423
scrambled egg and muffin ... 1	160g	1522	364
meat loaf ... baked	100g	835	200
meat see **individual types**			
meat spreads see **dips and spreads**			
meat substitutes ... Sanitarium ... B-B-Q links ... 2	85g	580	139
bologna ... 2 slices	54g	460	110
casserole mince ... 1/8 can	55g	180	43
country stew ... 1/2 can	200g	640	153
nut meat ... 2 slices	54g	420	100
nutolene ... 2 slices	54g	520	124
rediburger ... 2 slices	60g	420	100

	MASS	KJ	CAL
salad loaf ... 2 slices	72g	380	91
savoury pie ... 1/4 can	110g	810	194
soya loaf ... 2 slices	72g	560	134
Swiss rounds ... 1 pattie	110g	680	163
tender bits ... 1/6 can	72g	240	57
vegecuts ... 2 slices	72g	320	76
vegelinks ... 2	75g	410	98
vegetarian sausages ... 2	85g	460	110
Soy Feast ... burger mix	50g	705	168
mee grob (Thai)	100g	1525	364
melon ... bitter melon ... raw ... 1 av	126g	25	6
canteloupe/rockmelon ... raw			
flesh only ... 1 cup diced	165g	150	36
hairy melon ... raw ... 1 cup diced	130g	60	14
honeydew ... raw ... flesh only ... 1 cup diced	165g	215	51
watermelon ... raw ... flesh only ... 1 cup diced	195g	185	44

meringues see **cakes and pastries**

milk

	MASS	KJ	CAL
buttermilk ...	250ml	413	99
Healtheries ... powdered ... 3 tbsp	25g	418	100

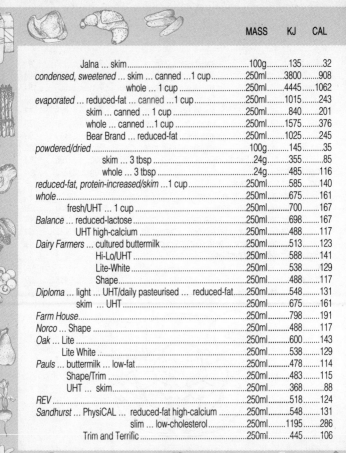

	MASS	KJ	CAL
Jalna ... skim	100g	135	32
condensed, sweetened ... skim ... canned ...1 cup	250ml	3800	908
whole ... 1 cup	250ml	4445	1062
evaporated ... reduced-fat ... canned ...1 cup	250ml	1015	243
skim ... canned ... 1 cup	250ml	840	201
whole ... canned ...1 cup	250ml	1575	376
Bear Brand ... reduced-fat	250ml	1025	245
powdered/dried	100g	145	35
skim ... 3 tbsp	24g	355	85
whole ... 3 tbsp	24g	485	116
reduced-fat, protein-increased/skim ...1 cup	250ml	585	140
whole	250ml	675	161
fresh/UHT ... 1 cup	250ml	700	167
Balance ... reduced-lactose	250ml	698	167
UHT high-calcium	250ml	488	117
Dairy Farmers ... cultured buttermilk	250ml	513	123
Hi-Lo/UHT	250ml	588	141
Lite-White	250ml	538	129
Shape	250ml	488	117
Diploma ... light ... UHT/daily pasteurised ... reduced-fat	250ml	548	131
skim ... UHT	250ml	675	161
Farm House	250ml	798	191
Norco ... Shape	250ml	488	117
Oak ... Lite	250ml	600	143
Lite White	250ml	538	129
Pauls ... buttermilk ... low-fat	250ml	478	114
Shape/Trim	250ml	483	115
UHT ... skim	250ml	368	88
REV	250ml	518	124
Sandhurst ... PhysiCAL ... reduced-fat high-calcium	250ml	548	131
slim ... low-cholesterol	250ml	1195	286
Trim and Terrific	250ml	445	106

	MASS	KJ	CAL
Skinny	250ml	408	98
White Gold ... modified	250ml	938	224
milk, buffalo	250ml	1075	257
milk, flavoured	300ml	1125	269
milk shake ... 1	340ml	1735	415
Akta-vite ... made up ... 15g + 200ml milk	760	182	
Berri Iced ... av all flavours	300ml	735	176
Big M ... av all flavours	300ml	966	231
Dairy Farmers ... Good One ... av all flavours	300ml	1155	276
Moove ... av all flavours	300ml	945	226
UHT Moove ... av all flavours	300ml	975	233
Healtheries ... carob drink ...2 tsp powder + 200ml milk	690	165	
Lift ... av all flavours	300ml	870	208
McDonald's ... thick shake ... 1	340ml	1150	275
Milo ... made up ... 20g + 200ml milk	930	222	
Norco ... av all flavours	300ml	990	237
Oak ... av all flavours	300ml	1140	272
Ovaltine ... made up ... 20g + 200ml milk	854	204	
light break ... 20g + 200ml water	355	85	
Pauls ... breaka dairy drink ... av all flavours	300ml	843	201
egg nog	250ml	728	174
go lite ... choc/coffee	300ml	585	140
Good One	300ml	909	217
shayks ... av all flavours	300ml	969	232
toot	300ml	792	189
UHT breaka ... av all flavours	300ml	912	218

Thirst-quenching should not cost you kilojoules. Milk-based drinks and even fruit juices should be regarded as food rather than liquid replacement. Herbal teas are a welcome refresher, good to drink without milk and with the added benefit of being caffeine-free. Remember that water is the best thirst-quencher.

	MASS	KJ	CAL
Spring Valley ... UHT ... Baco Luxury ... av all flavours	300ml	765	183
Sustagen	300ml	1410	337
Weight Watchers ... made up ... av all flavours	300ml	510	122
milk, goat's	250ml	700	167
Nanny Goat Lane/Simply Better	250ml	700	167
milk, human	250ml	738	176
milk, sheep's	250ml	1125	269
milk, soya bean see soya drink			
millet	100g	1350	323
Milo ... powder ... 1 tbsp	8g	136	33
see also milk, flavoured			
mince pies, fruit see pies, sweet			
mince see beef; lamb; pork			
mincemeat (fruit filling)	20g	235	56
mineral water see drinks, carbonated			
mint jelly ... Masterfoods	5g	55	13
miso ... 1 tbsp	20ml	170	41
mixed peel ... candied	100g	1325	317
molasses ... black	100g	900	215
light	100g	1075	257
Mongolian lamb ... Farmland ... uncooked ... 1 sv	200g	1140	272
mornay chicken ... Harvest	100g	262	63
mortadella see luncheon meat			
morwong ... battered, deep-fried	100g	870	208
crumbed, pan-fried	100g	835	200
steamed	100g	530	127
moussaka (Greek) ... fresh-cooked	100g	640	153
muesli bars see health-food bars			
muesli see breakfast cereals			
muffin mix ... Abundant Earth ... oatbran ... 1	60g	912	218
Green's ... banana ... 1	60g	778	186

	MASS	KJ	CAL
blueberry ... 1	60g	790	189
honey and walnut ... 1	60g	774	185
pumpkin 'n spice ... 1	60g	714	171
muffins ... 1	65g	600	143
Sara Lee ... blueberry ... 1	75g	1100	263
oatbran ... 1	75g	861	206
Tip Top ... apple strudel/spicy fruit ... 1	65g	640	153
English ... 1	67g	603	144
multigrain ... 1	67g	610	146
Weight Watchers ... 1	55g	511	122
mulberries ... flesh + seeds ... raw ... 1 cup	130g	160	38
mullet ... battered, deep-fried	100g	1225	293
floured, pan-fried	100g	860	206
steamed	100g	560	134
mulloway ... battered, deep-fried	100g	1000	239
crumbed, pan-fried	100g	800	191
steamed	100g	540	129
mung bean sprouts see *beans, mung*			
mushrooms ... Chinese	100g	1180	282
dried	100g	1150	275
raw ... 1 cup sliced	70g	70	17
sauteed in butter	100g	460	110
straw ... canned ... drained	100g	125	30
Edgell ... sliced ... in butter sauce	100g	190	45
Farmland ... no added salt	100g	130	31

With almost no fat, cholesterol, salt or sugar, and as a significant supplier of valuable dietary fibre, the mushroom is one of the dieter's allies in the fight against weight gain. Mushrooms are a rich source of vitamins, especially in the B-complex group including riboflavin, niacin, thiamin and pantothenic acid. They are also one of the very few vegetable sources of vitamin B_{12}.

	MASS	KJ	CAL
SPC ... sliced	100g	75	18
in butter sauce	100g	210	50
mushrooms, button see champignons			
mushrooms, oyster	100g	85	20
mussels ... boiled	100g	365	87
canned	100g	480	115
smoked ... canned in oil ... drained ... 1 cup	160g	1300	311
Admiral	100g	1030	246
John West	100g	859	205
mustard ... Masterfoods ... av all types	5g	25	6
mustard chicken ... Healthy Choice ... 1 sv	230g	943	225
mustard pickles see pickles			
mustard powder	5g	97	23
mutton curry with vegetables	100g	585	140
mutton stew with potatoes and onions see Irish stew			
nachos ... with cheese	100g	1280	306
nasi goreng ... Vesta ... 1 pkt made up ... 2 svs	214g	3143	751
nectarines ... raw ... 1 av	80g	115	27
nibbles see snack foods			
noodles ... egg ... boiled	100g	500	120
dried ... uncooked ... all types	100g	1540	368
nut meat see meat substitutes			
nuts see individual types of nuts; snack foods			
oat bran see breakfast cereals			
oatmeal/oats see breakfast cereals			
octopus see calamari			
offal see beef; lamb; veal			
oils ... all types	100g	3700	884
1 tbsp	12g	445	106
okra ... boiled ... 10 pods	100g	95	23

	MASS	KJ	CAL
raw ... 10 pods	111g	95	23
olives ... black	100g	830	198
green ... pickled	100g	535	128
Always Fresh ... herbed black	100g	516	123
sliced black	100g	830	198
spiced green	100g	394	94
omelette ... chicken (Chinese)	100g	895	214
Lebanese	100g	710	170
plain	100g	1040	249
prawn (Chinese)	100g	765	183
onions ... dried/flakes ... Dewcrisp ... easy-serve dried chopped	100g	240	57
fried ... average type	100g	1425	341
pickled ... 5 small	50g	65	16
Always Fresh ... sweet-and-sour/home-style	100g	280	67
Birds Eye ... chopped	100g	145	35
McCain	100g	142	34
onions, brown ... boiled ... 1 cup chopped	220g	250	60
raw ... 1	98g	100	24
onions, spring ... raw ... 1	14g	15	4
onions, white ... boiled ... 1	70g	85	20
raw ... 1 cup chopped	125g	140	33
orange juice see *fruit juices*			
orange peel, candied	100g	1325	317
orange ruff see *ruff, tommy/orange*			
oranges ... fresh ... raw ... 1 av	165g	190	45
navel ... 1 av	205g	255	61
valencia ... 1 av	225g	245	59
oriental beef with vegetable and rice ... Findus Lean Cuisine ... 1 sv	245g	1090	261
osso bucco (Italian)	100g	805	192
ouzo see *spirits*			
Ovaltine ... powder ... 1 tbsp	8g	105	25

	MASS	KJ	CAL
see also *milk, flavoured*			
oysters ... fresh ... 1 dozen	59g	180	43
fried in butter	100g	1000	239
smoked ... canned in oil ... drained ... 5	30g	260	62
Admiral	100g	850	203
John West	100g	950	227
pad thai (Thai)	100g	860	206
paella ... Vesta ... 1 pkt made up ... 2 svs	202g	2892	691
pancake mix ... Green's ... shake ... 1 sv ...			
banana/blueberry/apple cinnamon/original	50g	786	188
chocolate chip	50g	855	204
pancakes ... plain ... fresh-cooked ... 16 cm diam ... 1	80g	990	237
pandanus	100g	330	79
papaya see *pawpaw*			
pappadums ... raw	100g	1155	276

Curried Parsnip Soup

1 teaspoon oil
450 g peeled and sliced parsnips
1 onion, chopped
1 level teaspoon curry powder
850 ml water
1 vegetable stock cube

1 level teaspoon mango chutney
salt and pepper to taste
25 g skim milk powder
1 level teaspoon chopped fresh
  coriander (optional)

Heat oil in a large non-stick pan. Add parsnips and onion, cover and cook gently for 5 minutes. Stir in curry powder and cook for another minute. Add water, crumbled stock cube, chutney and seasoning. Bring to the boil and then simmer, covered, for 30 minutes. Remove from heat and blend until smooth. Mix milk powder with 2 tablespoons of water and stir into soup. Reheat gently. Garnish with chopped coriander to serve. Serves 4 at 525 kJ (125 Cal) per portion.

	MASS	KJ	CAL
parsley, common ... raw ... 10 sprigs	10g	5	1
parsley, continental ... raw ... 1 tbsp chopped	5g	5	1
parsnip ... boiled ... 1 cup chopped	150g	310	74
partridge ... roasted ... meat only	100g	890	213
passionfruit ... raw ... flesh only ... 1 av	21g	40	10
pasta ... dried ... uncooked ... av types	100g	1540	368
egg/spinach ... boiled ... 1 cup	200g	1090	261
white ... boiled ... 1 cup	180g	895	214
wholemeal ... boiled ... 1 cup	170g	928	222
Latina ... no egg, no cholesterol ... boiled ... all varieties	100g	720	172
Weight Watchers ... cooked ... av all types ... 1 sv	165g	777	186
see also specific types, e.g. *lasagna,* and individual meals, e.g. *macaroni cheese*			
pasta and sauce ... Continental ...			
creamy bacon carbonara ... 1 sv	123g	770	184
fettucini verdi ... 1 sv	120g	780	186
savoury tomato and onion ... 1 sv	120g	700	167
sour cream and chives ... 1 sv	118g	720	172
Continental vegetarian ... 1 sv ...			
creamy pomodora/creamy vegetable fontana	140g	600	143
karma vegetable curry	140g	570	136
sour cream and pumpkin	140g	620	148
pasticcio (Greek)	100g	645	154
pasties ... 1	165g	1820	435
Herbert Adams ... D-shaped pastie ... 1	175g	1603	383
vegetable pastie ... 1	175g	1488	356
Wedgwood ... party pastie ... 1	42g	474	113
pastry ... biscuit crust ... raw	100g	2180	521
choux ... baked	100g	1380	330
filo ... baked	100g	1560	373
raw	100g	1180	282

	MASS	KJ	CAL
flaky ... raw	100g	1695	405
puff ... baked	100g	1875	448
raw	100g	1515	362
shortcrust ... baked	100g	2045	489
raw	100g	1735	415
Pampas ... pizza bases ... raw	100g	1149	275
puff pastry sheets ... raw	100g	1471	352
shortcrust pastry sheets ... raw	100g	1590	380
sweet shortcrust tart shells ... 1 ... raw	23g	434	104
wholemeal pastry sheets ... raw	100g	1467	351
I & J ... superlight	100g	1490	356
pastry, Danish see *cakes and pastries*			
pastry mix ... Green's ... made up	50g	950	227
White Wings ... wholemeal ... not made up	100g	365	87
pâté ... chicken liver ... 1 tbsp	20g	105	25
pâté de fois ... av all brands	100g	1240	296
pavlova see *desserts and puddings*			
pawpaw ... canned	100g	275	65
fresh ... flesh only ... 1 cup diced	150g	185	44
glacé ... Winn	100g	1420	339
peaches ... canned ... artific. sweet. ... 1 cup slices + 40ml liquid	250g	263	63
drained ... 1 cup slices	210g	220	53

	MASS	KJ	CAL
in pear juice ... 1 cup slices	260g	440	105
drained ... 1 cup slices	210g	355	85
in syrup ... 1/2 peach + 25ml syrup	65g	140	33
drained ... 1/2 peach	40g	85	20
dried	100g	1130	270
stewed ... with sugar	100g	630	151
raw ... 1 peach	155g	185	44
stewed ... with sugar	100g	395	94
without sugar	100g	335	80
SPC ... in juice	100g	205	49
in syrup	100g	235	56
snak pak ... in juice	140g	282	67
lite	140g	253	60
Weight Watchers ... handy pack	100g	112	27

peanut butter see *dips and spreads*

peanut oil see *oils*

	MASS	KJ	CAL
peanuts ... choc-coated .. 1/4 cup	30g	705	168
raw ... 30	25g	590	141
roasted ... 30	25g	610	146

see also *snack foods*

	MASS	KJ	CAL
pear and peach quarters ... Goulburn Valley ... in fruit juice	100g	213	51
pears ... canned ... artific. sweet. ... 1/2 pear + 40 ml liquid	95g	105	25
drained ... 1/2 pear	55g	60	14
in pear juice ... drained ... 1/2 pear	55g	100	24
in syrup ... drained ... 1/2 pear	55g	135	32
dried	100g	1130	270
stewed ... with sugar	100g	630	151
raw ... stewed ... with sugar	100g	385	92
without sugar	100g	135	32
Goulburn Valley ... in fruit juice	100g	213	51
SPC ... in syrup	100g	250	60
lite	100g	180	43

	MASS	KJ	CAL
nutradiet ... artific. sweet. ... halves	100g	100	24
snak pak.. in juice	140g	275	66
lite ... in natural juice	140g	245	59
Weight Watchers ... artific. sweet. ... halves	100g	135	32
pears, brown skin ... raw ... 1 pear	145g	295	71
pears, Packhams Triumph ... raw ... 1 pear	235g	465	111
pears, Williams/Bartlett/Bon Chretien ... raw ... 1 pear	155g	275	66
pears, yellow-green skin ... raw ... 1 pear	205g	390	93
peas, green ... boiled ... 1 cup	165g	335	80
canned ... drained ... 1 cup	175g	440	105
dried ... boiled ... 1 cup	135g	260	62
frozen ... boiled ... 1 cup	160g	335	80
raw ... 1 cup	145g	360	86
split ... boiled ... 1/2 cup	90g	220	53
dried	100g	1455	348
Birds Eye ... frozen	100g	264	63
Edgell ... canned	100g	238	57
Farmland ... no added salt	100g	320	76
Golden Circle	100g	290	69
McCain	100g	310	74
baby	100g	293	70

	MASS	KJ	CAL
Watties	100g	270	65
peas, snow/sugar ... boiled ... 10 pods	30g	45	11
raw ... 10 pods	33g	45	11
pecan nuts ... snack-size sv	50g	1440	344
pepino ... raw ... flesh+seeds ... 1 av	123g	115	27
pepper ... ½ tsp	2g	25	6
pepperoni see *luncheon meat: salami*			
pepper steak ... Healthy Choice ... 1 sv	310g	1259	301
peppers ... boiled ... drained ... 1 sv	50g	40	10
immature, green (hot chilli) ... raw	100g	155	37
mature, red, inc seeds ... raw	100g	390	93
perch ... raw	100g	325	78
perch, northern pearl ... baked	100g	410	98
grilled	100g	400	96
poached	100g	395	94
raw	100g	320	76
smoked	100g	335	80
steamed	100g	350	84
persimmon ... raw ... flesh only ... 1	76g	210	50
pheasant ... roasted ... flesh only	100g	890	213
inc bone	100g	565	135
pickle	100g	640	153
dill ... 1 large	100g	45	11
gherkin ... 2 large	100g	57	14
mustard ... sour	20g	25	6
sweet	20g	95	23
Leggo's ... spreadable mustard/sweet mustard	20g	71	17
Masterfoods ... sweet mustard	5g	15	4
tomato	5g	20	5
pickle chow ... sour	100g	120	29
sweet	100g	485	116
pies, savoury ... beef ... family-size ... ¼	120g	1130	270

	MASS	KJ	CAL
individual-size ... 1	190g	1800	430
party-size ... 1	40g	465	111
fish	100g	540	129
pork ... 1	180g	2815	673
spinach (Lebanese)	100g	1215	290
steak and kidney ... 1	180g	2430	581
Farmland ... meat ... 1	90g	1030	246
Four'N Twenty ... chicken ... 1	175g	1768	423
light meat ... 1	175g	1594	381
meat ... 1	175g	1978	473
mexicana ... 1	175g	1855	443
steak and onion ... 1	175g	1925	460
Herbert Adams ... heritage meat ... 1	175g	1838	439
microwave light meat ... 1	175g	1594	381
party ... 1	50g	620	148
steak and onion ... 1	175g	1978	473
Munch 'n Crunch ... chicken and vegetable ... 1	150g	1515	362
pies, sweet ... apple ... fresh-baked ... whole	735g	7350	1757
fruit ... 1 small	150g	2330	557
fruit mince	100g	1140	272
fruit pie with pastry top	100g	755	180
lemon meringue	100g	1360	325
pecan	100g	1755	419
pumpkin	100g	885	212
Farmland ... apple ... frozen	100g	1005	240
Nanna's ... family ... apple ... 1/6 pie	100g	963	230
blackberry and apple ... 1/5 pie	100g	1095	262
tropical dessert ... 1/5 pie	100g	1300	311
Sara Lee ... apple pie ... 1/8 pie	75g	915	219
apricot cake pie ... 1/8 pie	65g	856	205

	MASS	KJ	CAL
hi pies ... apple ... 1/8 pie	100g	1054	252
mini apple-berry hi pie ... 1	150g	1833	438
pigeon/squab ... roasted	100g	960	229
pike ... raw	100g	375	90
pilchards ... canned in tomato sauce	100g	530	127
John West ... in tomato sauce	100g	580	139
pimientos ... canned ... solids + liquid ... 3 medium	100g	115	27
pine nuts/kernels ... raw ... 1 tbsp	14g	350	84
pineapple ... canned in heavy syrup ... 1 cup pieces	270g	965	231
drained ... 1 cup pieces	200g	700	167
in pineapple juice ... drained ... 1 slice	40g	75	18
glacé ... 1 ring	42g	555	133
raw ... flesh only ... 1 slice	110g	175	42
Golden Circle ... slices/pieces/crush	100g	345	82
slices/pieces ... unsweetened	100g	185	44
pineapple juice see *fruit juices*			
pistachio nuts ... shelled ... 25	15g	375	90
pizza ... commercial ... ham and pineapple ... 1/2	260g	2535	606
supreme ... 1/4	205g	1960	468
Farmland ... ham and pineapple	100g	910	217
supreme	100g	830	198
McCain ... cheese and bacon	500g	4900	1171
ham and pineapple	500g	4580	1095
microwave ham and pineapple	270g	2095	501

	MASS	KJ	CAL
microwave supreme	270g	2284	546
singles ham and pineapple	450g	3969	949
supreme	500g	4155	993
Pizza Hut ... Pan Pizza ... cheese ... 2 slices, av	210g	2184	522
Hawaiian ... 2 slices, av	250g	2450	586
super supreme ... 2 slices, av	286g	2846	680
supreme ... 2 slices, av	272g	2870	686
Thin 'n Crispy ... cheese ... 2 slices, av	158g	1818	435
Hawaiian ... 2 slices, av	198g	2030	485
super supreme ... 2 slices, av	234g	2434	582
supreme ... 2 slices, av	228g	2394	572
plaice ... crumbed, fried	100g	950	227
fried in batter	100g	1165	278
steamed ... with bones + skin	100g	210	50
without bones	100g	390	93
plantain ... boiled	100g	520	124
green ... raw	100g	475	114
ripe ... fried	100g	1125	269
plums ... fresh ... raw ... 1 av	110g	155	37
stewed ... with sugar	100g	295	71
without sugar	100g	135	32
red-fleshed/damson ... raw ... 1 av	77g	120	29
stewed ... with sugar	100g	295	71
wiithout sugar	100g	135	32
yellow-fleshed ... raw ... 1 av	70g	85	20
polenta ... dry	100g	2074	496
The Old Grain Mill	100g	1485	355
pomegranates ... fresh ... raw	100g	300	72
popcorn see *snack foods*			
pork			
barbecued (Chinese)	100g	995	238
boneless, average cut ... cooked ... lean ... 1 cup diced	190g	1350	323

	MASS	KJ	CAL
lean+fat ... 1 cup diced	181g	2255	539
butterfly steak ... grilled ... lean ... 1 av	100g	675	161
lean+fat ... 1 av	120g	1310	313
forequarter chops ... grilled ... lean ... 1 av	103g	780	186
lean+fat ... 1 av	144g	2070	495
leg ... baked/roast ... lean ... 1 boneless slice	31g	225	54
lean+fat ... 1 boneless slice	45g	635	152
leg steak ... grilled ... lean ... 1 av	82g	535	128
lean+fat ... 1 av	85g	615	147
medallion steak ... grilled ... lean ... 1 av	74g	580	139
lean+fat ... 1 av	95g	1230	294
mid-loin chop ... grilled ... lean ... 1 av	68g	495	118
lean+fat ... 1 av	101g	1535	367
mince ... cooked	100g	1055	252
trotters and tails ... boiled	100g	1160	277
pork buns	100g	1116	267
pork chop suey (Chinese)	100g	510	122
pork in plum sauce (Chinese)	100g	1025	245
pork noisettes ... Healthy Choice ... 1 sv	310g	977	234
pork pie see *pies, savoury*			
pork spare ribs in black-bean sauce (Chinese)	100g	835	200
pork, spit roast... Healthy Choice ... 1 sv	310g	1247	298
porridge see *breakfast cereals*			
port see *wines, fortified*			
potato cakes... deep-fried ... 1 av	95g	1285	306
McCain ... 1	100g	1355	324
potato chips ... commercial ... 1 cup	95g	975	233
French fries ... 1 cup		1135	271
home-made ... 10 chips	45g	360	86

Plan interesting meals. Organise low-kilojoule snacks ahead of time in case you feel tempted to nibble.

	MASS	KJ	CAL
Birds Eye ... Canola chips	100g	604	144
crinklecut chips	100g	582	139
country/crinkle slices	100g	604	144
French fries	100g	765	183
homestyle chips/oven fries	100g	591	141
Healthy Choice ... country cut fries	100g	630	151
potato crisps see *snack foods*			
potato gems ... Birds Eye	100g	660	158
potato n'sauce ... Green's ... cheddar cheese	100g	504	120
sour cream and clives	100g	510	122
potato scallops see *potato cakes*			
potatoes ... baked ... flesh only (not skin) ...			
1 med	100g	305	73
in jacket ... 1 med	120g	340	81
topped with cheese and bacon	100g	630	151
topped with sour cream and chives	100g	545	130
dehydrated ... made up	100g	390	93
not made up	100g	1500	359
Continental ... Deb ... plain/with onion ...1 pkt made up		1950	466
Edgell ... potato whip/with onion ... not made up	100g	1505	360
hash browns ... Birds Eye	100g	715	171
mashed ...+milk+butter ... ½ cup	120g	474	113
new ... canned ... drained ... 5 av	175g	415	99
peeled ... boiled ... 1 av	60g	160	38
Admiral ... whole new/with mint	100g	225	54
SPC ... new	100g	170	41
peeled ... boiled ... 1 med	100g	270	65
roasted ... 2 med halves	85g	380	91
scalloped	100g	435	104
Admiral ... with cheese sauce	100g	303	72

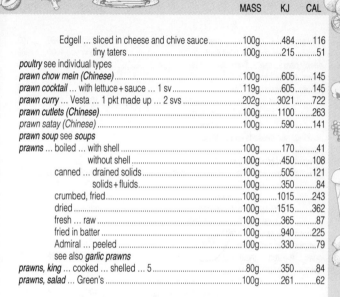

	MASS	KJ	CAL
Edgell ... sliced in cheese and chive sauce	100g	484	116
tiny taters	100g	215	51
poultry see individual types			
prawn chow mein (Chinese)	100g	605	145
prawn cocktail ... with lettuce + sauce ... 1 sv	119g	605	145
prawn curry ... Vesta ... 1 pkt made up ... 2 svs	202g	3021	722
prawn cutlets (Chinese)	100g	1100	263
prawn satay (Chinese)	100g	590	141
prawn soup see *soups*			
prawns ... boiled ... with shell	100g	170	41
without shell	100g	450	108
canned ... drained solids	100g	505	121
solids + fluids	100g	350	84
crumbed, fried	100g	1015	243
dried	100g	1515	362
fresh ... raw	100g	365	87
fried in batter	100g	940	225
Admiral ... peeled	100g	330	79
see also *garlic prawns*			
prawns, king ... cooked ... shelled ... 5	80g	350	84
prawns, salad ... Green's	100g	261	62

	MASS	KJ	CAL
prawns, school ... cooked ... shelled ... 1 cup	135g	430	103
prawns, sweet-and-sour (Chinese)	100g	1600	382
prickly pear ... raw ... flesh only ... 1 av	86g	145	35
prosciutto see *ham*			
prunes ... dessert	100g	780	186
dried	100g	1065	255
stewed ... with sugar	100g	740	177
without sugar	100g	500	120
puddings see *desserts and puddings*			
pumello	100g	200	48
pumpernickel see *bread: loaves*			
pumpkin ... average type ... boiled ... 1 cup pieces	170g	300	72
butternut ... boiled	100g	194	46
mashed ... 1 cup	245g	475	114
golden nugget ... boiled ... ½	130g	165	39
Queensland blue ... boiled ... 1 cup pieces	170g	350	84
pumpkin scones see *scones*			
pumpkin soup see *soups*			
quail ... roasted ... meat only	100g	728	174
quiche ... lorraine ... 1 sv	150g	2435	582
Sara Lee ... light ... ham, tomato, fetta	100g	665	159
spinach and ricotta	100g	644	154
lorraine ... ⅙	100g	1115	266
vegetable ... ⅙	100g	980	234
quinces ... canned	100g	350	84
raw ... flesh only ... 1 av	219g	440	105
stewed with sugar	100g	350	84
rabbit ... baked	100g	855	204
stewed	100g	785	188
radish ... oriental ... raw ... 1 cup sliced	95g	70	17
red ... raw ... 1 av	15g	10	2

	MASS	KJ	CAL
white ... raw	60g	60	14
raisin bread see *bread*			
raisins ... dried	30g	350	84
rambutan ... 1 av	14g	15	4
raspberries ... canned in juice	100g	200	48
in syrup	100g	425	102
fresh	100g	240	57
stewed ... with sugar	100g	290	69
without sugar	100g	200	48
John West ... in syrup	100g	295	71
ratatouille ...SPC	100g	105	25
ravioli ... commercial ... av all brands ... 1 cup	265g	1450	347
ravioli Bolognese ... Griffs	100g	1095	262
Heinz ... supersnack	100g	410	98
red emperor ... baked	100g	410	98
grilled	100g	400	96
poached	100g	395	94
raw	100g	320	76
smoked	100g	335	80
steamed	100g	350	84
red pepper see *capsicum*			
redcurrant jelly ... 1 tsp	5ml	55	13
redcurrants	100g	215	51
relish see *chutney; dips and spreads*			
rhubarb ... stewed ... with sugar	100g	270	65
without sugar ... 1 sv	120g	30	7
ribena ... undiluted	100g	975	233
rice			
basmati ... raw	100g	1500	359
brown ... boiled ... 1 cup	180g	1135	271

Brown rice has a higher dietary fibre content than white rice as it has had only the inedible husk removed, leaving the bran layers and germ intact.

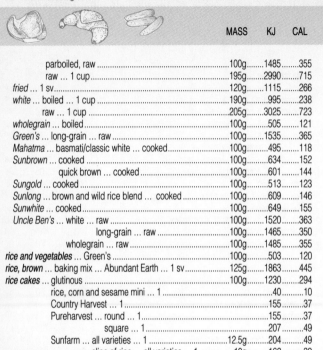

	MASS	KJ	CAL
parboiled, raw	100g	1485	355
raw ... 1 cup	195g	2990	715
fried ... 1 sv	120g	1115	266
white ... boiled ... 1 cup	190g	995	238
raw ... 1 cup	205g	3025	723
wholegrain ... boiled	100g	505	121
Green's ... long-grain ... raw	100g	1535	365
Mahatma ... basmati/classic white ... cooked	100g	495	118
Sunbrown ... cooked	100g	634	152
quick brown ... cooked	100g	601	144
Sungold ... cooked	100g	513	123
Sunlong ... brown and wild rice blend ... cooked	100g	609	146
Sunwhite ... cooked	100g	649	155
Uncle Ben's ... white ... raw	100g	1520	363
long-grain ... raw	100g	1465	350
wholegrain ... raw	100g	1485	355
rice and vegetables ... Green's	100g	503	120
rice, brown ... baking mix ... Abundant Earth ... 1 sv	125g	1863	445
rice cakes ... glutinous	100g	1230	294
rice, corn and sesame mini ... 1		40	10
Country Harvest ... 1		155	37
Pureharvest ... round ... 1		155	37
square ... 1		207	49
Sunfarm ... all varieties ... 1	12.5g	204	49
slice of rice ... all varieties ... 1	10g	162	39
rice crackers see *biscuits: Premier Japan*			
rice drink... Pureharvest Aussie Dream Natural	250ml	658	157
rice flakes, wholegrain ... Lowan Whole Foods	100g	1505	360
rice pudding see *desserts and puddings*			
rice salad see *salads*			
rice, savoury ... Continental ... Rices of the World ...			
4-sv pack ... made up ... Indian		2180	521

	MASS	KJ	CAL
Thai		2010	480
McCain ... fried rice	350g	2219	530
Uncle Ben's ... 4-sv pack ... made up ...			
chicken and vegetable		2842	679
green bean and almond		3634	869
tomato and herb		3033	725

rissoles, beef see *beef rissoles*
rock cakes see *cakes and pastries*
rockmelon see *melon*

	MASS	KJ	CAL
roe ... cod ... fried	100g	845	202
raw	100g	475	114

rolls see *bread: rolls*

	MASS	KJ	CAL
ruff, tommy/orange ... baked	100g	410	98
grilled	100g	400	96
poached	100g	395	94
raw	100g	320	76
smoked	100g	335	80
steamed	100g	350	84

rum see *spirits*
rump steak (fresh-cooked) see *beef*

	MASS	KJ	CAL
rusks ... Dutch	100g	1620	387
plain/wholemeal	100g	1725	412

rye bread see *bread: loaves*
rye flour see *flour, rye*

	MASS	KJ	CAL
rye meal	100g	1400	335

saccharin see *sugar substitutes*

For a dressing providing only 20 kJ (5 Cal) for four servings, try combining half a clove of garlic (crushed) with 3 tablespoons of apple juice and 1 tablespoon of red wine vinegar. Leave the mixture for 30 minutes before straining and discarding the garlic if desired.

	MASS	KJ	CAL
safflower oil	100g	3700	884
sago ... dry	100g	1500	359
*salad dressing** ... blue cheese ...Bertolli	20ml	376	90
Hain ... low-energy/no oil	20ml	61	15
coleslaw ... Fountain ... Salad Magic ... no cholesterol	20ml	215	51
Kraft	20ml	340	81
light	20ml	45	11
Praise	20ml	338	81
light	20ml	236	56
French (vinaigrette) ... av all brands	20ml	222	53
Fountain ... Salad Magic ... no oil	20ml	28	7
Hain ... creamy	20ml	332	79
spicy	20ml	299	71
Kraft	20ml	204	49
light	20ml	38	9
Praise	20ml	172	41
light	20ml	47	11
Weight Watchers ... salad singles	20ml	14	3
herb and garlic ... Fountain ... Salad Magic ... no oil	20ml	34	8
Hain ... low-energy/no oil	20ml	4	1
Kraft	20ml	225	54
Italian ... Best Foods ... low-energy/no oil	20ml	6	1
Fountain ... Salad Magic ... no oil	20ml	54	13
Hain	20ml	299	71
Kraft	20ml	248	59
light	20ml	5	1
Praise	20ml	158	38
light	20ml	34	8
Weight Watchers ... salad singles	20ml	24	6
Miracle Whip ... Kraft	20ml	420	100
Thousand Island ... Hain	20ml	286	68

*One tablespoon of dressing equals approximately 20 ml.

	MASS	KJ	CAL
low-energy/no oil	20ml	44	11
Kraft	20ml	321	77
Tangy Citrus ... Hain	20ml	299	71
salads ... bean ... commercial ... 1 cup	210g	1160	277
coleslaw ... 1 cup	200g	795	190
pasta	100g	1590	380
potato ... canned ... 1 cup	180g	900	215
commercial ... 1 cup	180g	815	195
rice	100g	2175	520
tabouli (Lebanese)	100g	610	146
waldorf	100g	3300	789
Heinz ... picnic pack/potato	100g	390	93
Masterfoods ... bean 'n' corn	100g	410	98
mixed beans	100g	225	54
mixed veg/potato/rice	100g	480	115
tropical	100g	360	86
zucchini	100g	170	41
salami see *luncheon meat*			
salmon ... baked	100g	760	182
canned in brine ... pink ... drained ... 1 cup	210g	1290	308
red ... drained ... 1 cup	210g	1710	409
raw	100g	905	216

Salmon and Pasta Salad

30 g large uncooked macaroni
1 45-g egg, hard boiled
2 lettuce leaves, torn
60 g red salmon, flaked

1 Lebanese cucumber or ½ regular cucumber, sliced
¼ teaspoon dried thyme
1 tablespoon oil-free French dressing

Cook macaroni in boiling salted water. Drain and set aside. Cool the egg, shell and quarter and add to lettuce with salmon and cucumber. Toss with macaroni to combine. Whisk the thyme with French dressing and pour over salad, tossing gently before serving immediately. Serves 1 at 1290 kJ (310 Cal).

	MASS	KJ	CAL
smoked ... 1 slice	25g	140	33
steamed	100g	825	197
inc bones + skin	100g	665	159
Atlantic salmon ... raw	100g	755	180
Australian salmon ... canned in brine ... drained ... 1 cup	210g	1530	366
fried	100g	845	202
raw	100g	475	114
smoked flavour ... Greenseas	100g	1130	270
pink salmon ... Ally ... no added salt ... drained	100g	650	155
Farmland ... no added salt ... drained	100g	620	148
Green's ... drained	100g	570	136
red salmon ... Farmland ... no added salt	100g	680	163
John West	100g	704	168
medium red	100g	700	167
salt, table	100g	0	0
saltimbocca (Italian)	100g	915	219
samosas (stuffed with minced lamb)	100g	2390	571
sandwiches ... (two slices bread, two tsp butter; all salad includes 1 tsp mayonnaise)			
beef German/Strasbourg/egg + lettuce ... 1		1295	310
cheese ... grated tasty ... 1		1230	294
processed slice ... 1		1170	280
cheese + salad ... grated tasty ... 1		1430	342
processed slice ... 1		1370	327
chicken + salad ... 1		1350	323
cream cheese + dried apricots + nuts ... 1		1805	431
ham ... (1 slice) ... 1		1110	265
ham + salad ... 1		1310	313
ham, salad + cheese ... 1		1580	378
open salad on rye ... 1		1270	304
pocket pita (buttered) + salad ... 1		1520	363

	MASS	KJ	CAL
roast beef/pork (1 slice) ... 1		1160	277
salad without meat/salad roll ... 1		1100	263
tomato ... 1		940	225
tuna+salad ... 1		1240	296
vegemite ... 1		900	215

Sanitarium meat analogues see *meat substitutes*

	MASS	KJ	CAL
sardines ... canned ... in brine	100g	820	196
in oil	100g	1285	307
drained ... 5 small	75g	715	171
in tomato sauce	100g	740	177
raw	100g	563	135
Admiral ... cutlets ... with green chilli	100g	1080	258
in barbecue sauce	100g	674	161
John West ... Scottish in oil... drained	100g	835	200
Scottish in tomato ... drained	100g	914	218
King Oscar ... oil pack ... drained	85g	1090	261
tomato pack/mustard pack	105g	1005	240

sauces, savoury*

	MASS	KJ	CAL
barbecue	20ml	75	18
bearnaise ... prepared with milk + butter	20ml	230	55
Bolognese	20ml	115	27
dried mix	20g	325	78

*One tablespoon of sauce equals approximately 20 ml.

	MASS	KJ	CAL
brown onion ... dried mix	20g	310	74
cheese	20ml	150	36
chilli ... 1 tbsp	20ml	20	5
chilli tomato	20ml	85	20
curry ... dried mix	20g	385	92
fish	20ml	50	12
hollandaise ... dried mix reconst. with water	20ml	465	111
using milk + butter/butterfat	20ml	230	55
meat	20ml	215	51
mushroom ... dried mix	20ml	300	72
oyster	20ml	70	17
parsley	20ml	155	37
soya	20ml	55	13
sweet-and-sour	20ml	110	26
tartare	20ml	420	100
tomato ... av all brands	20ml	75	18
no added salt ... White Crow	20ml	80	19
white	20ml	135	32
dried mix	20g	335	80
worcestershire	20ml	65	16
Cornwell's ... mint/chick mint	20ml	75	18
plum	20ml	115	27
soy	20ml	45	11
steak/worcestershire/Lancashire relish	20ml	100	24
sweet-and-sour	20ml	170	41
Dolmio ... chunky ... eggplant and shallots/ onion and mushroom	100g	206	49
provinciale ... carbonara	100g	504	120

Eating five small meals a day stimulates the body's metabolism and helps burn up extra kilojoules. Munching between meals is only a problem if you snack on biscuits, sweets, pastries, chocolate and other foods high in fat or sugar.

	MASS	KJ	CAL
chicken cacciatore/ seafood marinara	100g	208	50
traditional ... capsicum/mushroom	100g	197	47
spicy/tomato and basil	100g	212	51
Eastern Feast ... black bean	100g	350	84
mild Thai curry	100g	426	102
sweet and sour/honey and sesame	100g	467	112
ETA ... barbeque	20ml	150	36
Fountain ... fruit chutney	30g	260	62
mild chilli	30ml	85	20
mint	30ml	95	23
satay	30ml	275	66
teriyaki marinade and baste	30ml	155	37
Gravox ... brown onion and garlic sauce mix ... made up	60ml	85	20
creamy apricot and mango sauce mix ... made up	60ml	205	49
pepper sauce/white sauce mix ... made up	60ml	183	44
Heinz ... tomato ketchup/tomato sauce	20ml	95	23
Kan Tong ... lemon and honey/satay	100g	291	70
sweet-and-sour	100g	436	104
Kraft ... tartare ... 1 tbsp	20ml	270	65
Lawry's ... marinade mix ... per pack ... beef		350	84
chicken		370	88
Masterfoods ... tartare ... 1 tbsp	20g	484	116
Paul Newman's ... marinara spaghetti/mushroom spaghetti	100g	235	56
sockarooni spaghetti	100g	185	44
Raguletto ... lighter style ... Basilico/parmigiana pasta	100g	152	36
Calabrese spicy pasta	100g	170	41
Rosella ... herbed chicken with wine	100g	305	73
oriental chicken	100g	220	53
Uncle Ben's ... apricot chicken/savoury steak	100g	244	58
devilled sausages	100g	190	45
Hawaiian sweet-and-sour	100g	402	96

	MASS	KJ	CAL
tuna mornay	100g	302	72
Weekday Gourmet ... creamy wine and mushroom/			
Indonesian satay	100g	533	127
Mexican taco	100g	164	39
mild Indian curry	100g	324	77
parmigiana	100g	206	49
Weight Watchers ... pasta sauce	100g	200	48
tomato sauce	15ml	39	9
White Wings ... bechamel sauce mix	20ml	10	2
dianne sauce mix	20ml	60	14
pepper sauce mix	20ml	35	8
see also *gravy*			
sauces, sweet ... apple	20ml	70	17
chocolate topping	20ml	163	39
cranberry ... canned ... sweetened	20ml	125	30
fruit flavours, av	20ml	150	36
low-joule topping ... Cottees	20ml	35	8
maple syrup	20ml	50	12
topping ... flavoured	20ml	115	27
white	20ml	155	37
sauerkraut ... canned	100g	80	19
Edgell	100g	95	23
sausage rolls ... av take-away ... 1	130g	1560	373

	MASS	KJ	CAL
party size ... 1	40g	505	121
Four 'N Twenty/Wedgwood ... jumbo ... 1	115g	1460	349
large ... 1	82g	984	235
Herbert Adams ... 1	38g	454	109
Nanna's ... 1	29g	321	77
sausages ... beef ... fried ... 2	120g	1350	323
grilled ... 2	120g	1550	370
liver	100g	1115	266
pork ... fried ... 2	120g	1580	378
grilled ... 2	120g	1620	387
saveloys see *frankfurters*			
savoury mince ... canned ... av all brands	100g	755	180
savoury noodles ... Tandaco ... one-pan dinner ... 1/4 pkt	50g	675	161
scallops ... cooked ... 1 cup	160g	705	168
raw ... 5	65g	145	35
scampi ... fried	100g	1015	243
schnitzel see *chicken schnitzel*; *veal schnitzel*			
scone mix ... White Wings ... plain	100g	255	61
wholemeal	100g	230	55
scones ... 1	40g	580	139
cheese ... 1	45g	594	142
fruit ... 1	50g	668	160
plain ... commercial ... 1	50g	565	135
home-made ... 1	40g	580	139
pumpkin ... 1	40g	584	140
sultana ... 1	50g	775	185
wholemeal ... 1	50g	740	177
wholemeal ... 1	45g	616	147
scotch eggs	100g	1160	277

Be prepared to accept that you may occasionally break your diet. At these times aim to maintain a constant weight.

			MASS	KJ	CAL

sea perch ... fried .... 100g 905 216

steamed .... 100g 385 92

seafood ... Admiral ... seafood mix .... 100g 480 115

I & J ... prawn caravelles .... 100g 922 220

sea cakes ... standard/tuna .... 100g 535 128

sea shanties .... 100g 930 222

see also individual types e.g. *crab*

seakale see *silver beet*

seasoned coating mix ... Tandaco ... chicken .... 100g 1225 293

fish/schnitzel .... 100g 1365 326

southern fried chicken .... 100g 1390 332

seasonings ... Continental ... hotpot casserole base ... per pack ...

curry 1854 443

French onion 1259 301

mushroom 1359 325

savoury 1377 329

sweet-and-sour 2126 508

tomato provencale 1253 299

Kellogg's ... cornflake crumbs/seasoned .... 100g 1580 378

self-raising flour see *flour, wheat*

semolina see *breakfast cereals*

sesame seeds ... 1 tsp .... 4g 95 23

shallots ... boiled ... 2 bulbs .... 12g 10 2

raw ... 2 bulbs .... 12g 10 2

shepherds pie ... home-made .... 100g 495 118

sherry see *wines, fortified*

shish kebab (Lebanese) .... 100g 790 189

shortbread see *biscuits*

shortening see *butter; lard; margarine*

shrimps ... boiled ... with shell .... 100g 165 39

without shell .... 100g 365 87

shrimps ... canned ... drained solids .... 100g 505 121

	MASS	KJ	CAL
solids + fluids	100g	350	84
crumbed, fried	100g	1015	243
dried	100g	1035	247
fried in batter	100g	940	225
frozen ... without shell	100g	310	74
raw	100g	400	96
King Oscar ... in brine	100g	400	96
silver beet ... boiled ... 1 cup chopped	115g	70	17
dehydrated	100g	1300	311
raw ... 1 cup chopped	45g	25	6
silverside see *beef*			
Singapore noodles ... Green's	100g	421	101
sirloin see *beef*			
skate ... fried in batter	100g	830	198
skordalia (Greek) see *dips and spreads*			
snack foods ... beer nuts ... av all brands	100g	2330	557
burger rings	100g	2090	500
cashew nuts ... salted ... av all brands	100g	2555	611
CC's tasty cheese ... Chefs Choice	100g	2080	497
cheese things	100g	2130	509
cheezels ... cheese and bacon flavour	100g	2240	535
chips/crisps ... flavoured ... 1 small pkt	25g	540	129
plain ... 1 small pkt	25g	525	125
chocolate-covered nuts	30g	670	160
corn chips ... flavoured ... 1 pkt	25g	520	124
toasted ... 1 pkt	25g	495	118
Lites ... lightly salted crisps	100g	2210	528
nutcrackers	100g	1840	440
nuts, mixed ... av all brands	100g	2440	583
peanuts ... salted ... av all brands	100g	2340	559
popcorn ... regular ... 1 cup	8g	155	37
sugar-coated	30g	2190	523

	MASS	KJ	CAL
pork rind ... 1 pkt	25g	510	122
potato straws ... flavoured ... 1 pkt	25g	730	174
plain ... 1 pkt	25g	755	180
pretzels ... 20 8-cm sticks	12g	185	44
twisties ... cheese	100g	2080	497
chicken	100g	2060	492
ETA ... mixed nuts ... salted	100g	2545	608
peanuts ... granulated/crushed	100g	2365	565
roasted	100g	2475	592
salted	100g	2440	583
Farmland ... beer nuts/cashews/roasted peanuts ... no added salt	100g	2640	631
mixed nuts	100g	2500	598
potato chips ... wrinkled ... no added salt	100g	2365	565
Fullers ... popping corn ... cooked in oil	100g	1605	384
McCain ... super crisps	100g	1070	256
Smith's ... Original Crinkle Cut Crisps	100g	2290	547
Sunburst ... bacon rings/ollos	100g	2180	521
Uncle Toby's ... le snak ... cheese spread ... in 1 pack		190	45
crispbreads (all flavours) ... in 1 pack		170	41
roll ups ... av all varieties ... 1 roll		235	56
snapper ... battered, deep-fried	100g	855	204
crumbed, pan-fried	100g	835	200
steamed	100g	510	122
snapper, red ... fried	100g	905	216
steamed	100g	385	92
snow peas see *peas, snow/sugar*			
soda water see *drinks, carbonated*			
sole ... baked	100g	845	202

	MASS	KJ	CAL
raw	100g	375	90
sole, lemon ... fried	100g	905	216
inc bones	100g	715	171
raw	100g	345	82
steamed	100g	385	92
inc bones	100g	270	65
soups			
chicken galanga soup (Thai)	100g	470	112
prawn (Thai)	100g	170	41
Alevita ... carrot/thick vegetable ... made up ... ½ sachet	250ml	370	88
spring vegetable ... made up ... ½ sachet	250ml	110	26
tomato ... made up ... ½ sachet	250ml	310	74
tomato and vegetable ... made up ... ½ sachet	250ml	325	78
Campbell's ... creamy all-natural soups ... diluted with ½ milk ½ water...			
asparagus/sweet potato	100g	318	76
corn	100g	244	58
garden tomato	100g	116	28
garden vegetable	100g	151	36
pumpkin	100g	192	46
chunky soups ... consumed undiluted ...			
beef/ham and pea	100g	330	79
chicken	100g	246	59
chicken and pasta/stockpot	100g	252	60
minestrone	100g	260	62
diluted with equal quantity of water ...			
beef consomme	100g	46	11
chicken vegetable	100g	112	27
old-fashioned stockpot	100g	133	32
split pea with ham	100g	270	65
tomato/italian tomato	100g	106	25
vegetable	100g	125	30

	MASS	KJ	CAL
diluted with ½ milk ½ water ...			
cream of chicken	100g	235	56
cream of chicken and corn/mushroom			
and bacon/broccoli and cheese	100g	225	54
cream of celery	100g	229	55
Continental ... packet soups ... made up with water ...			
cup-a-soup ... 1 sachet made up ...			
Chinese chicken and sweet corn		270	65
cream of celery		335	80
Indonesian tomato and beef		296	71
pea and ham		339	81
Singaporean golden vegetable		293	70
tomato		324	77
cup-a-soup salt-reduced ... 1 sachet made up ...			
chicken noodle		170	40
cream of mushroom		365	87
hearty beef		225	54
cup-a-soup special ... 1 sachet made up ...			
creamy lemon chicken with rice		580	139
creamy mushroom		397	95
seafood bisque		605	145
vegetable and beef		466	111
lots-a-noodles ... 1 sachet made up ...			
barbecue chicken		404	96
beef		490	117
Chinese golden chicken and corn		610	146
mild curry/tomato		508	121
vegetable		455	109
slim-a-soup ... 1 sachet made up ...			
chicken Florentine		166	40
chicken with wholemeal croutons/			
beef and tomato		159	38

	MASS	KJ	CAL
garden broccoli		168	40
garden vegetable		136	33
mild Malay chicken curry/			
mushroom and chives		156	37
tomato and herb		151	36
standard 1-litre ... 1 pack (4 svs) ... not made up ...			
cheese and leek		1045	250
chicken noodle		748	179
Dutch curry and rice ...			
salt-reduced		1152	275
tomato		1207	288
Country Cup ... instant ... 1 sachet made up ...			
chicken		527	126
pea and ham		492	118
pumpkin		393	94
tomato/vegetable		400	96
instant noodles ... 1 sachet made up ...			
chicken and corn/tomato		456	109
beef		447	107
instant premium ... 1 sachet made up ...			
pumpkin		375	90
seafood		381	91
tomato		470	112
trim soup ... 1 sachet made up ...			
chicken		192	46
chicken noodle		206	49
tomato/vegetable		188	45
Healthy Choice ... pumpkin and tortellini ... 1 sv	320g	992	237
Heinz ... all natural ... diluted with water ...			
tomato and basil	100g	145	35
veal and rice	100g	160	38
chunky pot ... bacon and tomato	100g	140	33

	MASS	KJ	CAL
spring lamb	100g	420	100
tortellini beef	100g	315	75
classics ... diluted with milk ...			
chicken supreme	100ml	345	82
seafood bisque	100ml	400g	96
consumed undiluted ... chicken and vegetable	100ml	105	25
pea with ham	100ml	205	49
tomato	100ml	125	30
tomato and bacon	100ml	145	35
vegetable beef	100ml	155	37
creamy condensed ... diluted with milk and water ...			
asparagus	100ml	250	60
chicken and asparagus	100ml	230	55
chicken and mushroom/			
pumpkin/seafood	100ml	260	62
main-course soup ... consumed undiluted ...			
chicken and corn	100ml	225	54
chunky beef and vegetables	100ml	240	57
ready-to serve soup for one ... consumed undiluted ...			
beef and vegetable/			
minestrone	100ml	175	42
creamy chicken	100ml	255	61
Maggi ... purees ... reconstituted with water ...			
carrot ... 1 sv	100ml	130	31
vegetable ... 1 sv	100ml	140	33
thick soups ... reconstituted with water ...			
av all varieties	100ml	110	26
country potato with beef/			
farmhouse stockpot	100ml	165	39
thin soups ... reconstituted with water ...			
chicken noodle/French onion	100ml	70	17
spring vegetable	100ml	45	11

	MASS	KJ	CAL
Rosella ... diluted with water ...			
beef goulash/chicken and vegetable ... 1 sv	220g	324	77
cream of chicken ... salt-reduced ... 1 sv	220g	341	82
cream of mushroom ... 1 sv	220g	360	86
pea and ham ... 1 sv	220g	528	126
spring vegetable ... 1 sv	220g	224	54
tomato ... salt-reduced ... 1 sv	220g	286	68
vegetable beef ... 1 sv	220g	271	65
soups in glass ...			
creamy chicken and corn ... 1 sv	375g	558	133
tomato, corn and capsicum ... 1 sv	375g	488	117
Weight Watchers ... condensed ... tomato/chicken/minestrone/			
pumpkin	100ml	95	23
vegetable	100ml	90	22
instant ... 1 sachet ...			
broccoli and asparagus	200ml	70	17
chicken, wholemeal			
croutons	200ml	85	20
chicken noodle	200ml	80	19
zesty tomato	200ml	65	16
White Wings ... trim soup ... 1 sachet made up ...			
chicken/beef		185	44

Soya Milk Health Drink

1½ cups vanilla-flavoured soya milk	8 unblanched almonds
2 tablespoons millet flakes	1 tablespoon liquid rice malt (optional)
2 tablespoons oat bran	2 small pears, peeled and quartered but
2 tablespoons fresh wheatgerm	left uncored (for extra fibre and nutrients)
2 tablespoons soy lecithin	dash of cinnamon to garnish

Place all ingredients except the cinnamon in a blender. Blend until smooth. Add extra soya milk if too thick. Pour into chilled glasses and sprinkle with cinnamon. Serves 2.

	MASS	KJ	CAL
chicken noodle		205	49
tomato		180	43
sour cream see *cream, sour*			
souvlakia (Greek)	100g	830	198
soya bean curd see *tofu*			
soya bean milk see *soya drink*			
soya bean oil	100g	3700	884
soya beans see *beans, soya*			
soya burgers ... tempeh	100g	860	205
soya drink ... soya bean milk	250ml	412	98
Berri ... soy drink ... all flavours	250ml	750	179
Ideal Dairy ... soy fresh ... chocolate	250ml	820	196
low-fat	250ml	465	111
natural	250ml	680	163
Pureharvest ... Aussie natural soy	250ml	575	137
Aussie vanilla soy	250ml	663	158
Sanitarium ... so good ... plain	250ml	650	155
lite	250ml	450	108
all other flavours	250ml	800	191
Sungold	250ml	685	164
Vitafresh ... soy drink	100ml	185	44
Vitasoy ... natural soy drink	250ml	640	153
soya flour see *flour, soya*			
soya sauce see *sauces, savoury*			

	MASS	KJ	CAL
spaghetti ... Edgell... curried/in tomato sauce and cheese	100g	332	79
quick and healthy	100g	231	55
Heinz ... Bolognese	100g	220	53
spaghetti in tomato sauce and cheese/ salt-reduced	100g	255	61
SPC	100g	305	73
spaghetti and meatballs ... Kraft	100g	415	99
spaghetti Bolognese	100g	535	128
Healthy Choice ... 1 sv	210g	1230	294
Heinz	100g	310	74
McCain	400g	2256	539
spaghetti marinara	100g	545	130
spaghetti Napoletana	100g	485	116
spaghetti sauce with meatballs ... Campbell's	150g	710	170
spaghetti with beef and mushroom sauce ... Findus Lean Cuisine ... 1 sv	325g	1255	300
spanakopita (Greek)	100g	1235	295
spices, dried ... alllspice/anise seeds/caraway seeds/chilli powder/chives/cinnamon/cloves/coriander/ cummin/curry powder/dill/fenugreek/oregano/ paprika/rosemary/turmeric ... 1 tsp	5g	65	16
1 pinch		5	1
spinach ... Chinese/common variety ... boiled ... 1 cup chopped	145g	115	27
raw ... 1 cup chopped	30g	20	5
spinach and lamb curry... Griffs ... 1 sv	400g	1669	399
spinach pie (Lebanese) see *pies, savoury*			
spirits ... brandy	30ml	200	48
gin	30ml	290	69
ouzo	30ml	345	82
rum	30ml	420	100
vermouth ... dry	100g	545	130

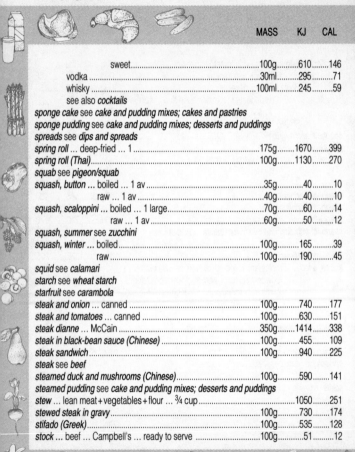

	MASS	KJ	CAL
sweet	100g	610	146
vodka	30ml	295	71
whisky	100ml	245	59
see also *cocktails*			
sponge cake see cake and pudding mixes; cakes and pastries			
sponge pudding see cake and pudding mixes; desserts and puddings			
spreads see dips and spreads			
spring roll ... deep-fried ... 1	175g	1670	399
spring roll (Thai)	100g	1130	270
squab see pigeon/squab			
squash, button ... boiled ... 1 av	35g	40	10
raw ... 1 av	40g	40	10
squash, scaloppini ... boiled ... 1 large	70g	60	14
raw ... 1 av	60g	50	12
squash, summer see zucchini			
squash, winter ... boiled	100g	165	39
raw	100g	190	45
squid see calamari			
starch see wheat starch			
starfruit see carambola			
steak and onion ... canned	100g	740	177
steak and tomatoes ... canned	100g	630	151
steak dianne ... McCain	350g	1414	338
steak in black-bean sauce (Chinese)	100g	455	109
steak sandwich	100g	940	225
steak see beef			
steamed duck and mushrooms (Chinese)	100g	590	141
steamed pudding see cake and pudding mixes; desserts and puddings			
stew ... lean meat + vegetables + flour ... ¾ cup		1050	251
stewed steak in gravy	100g	730	174
stifado (Greek)	100g	535	128
stock ... beef ... Campbell's ... ready to serve	100g	51	12

	MASS	KJ	CAL
Maggi ... recons. with water	100g	40	10
chicken ... Campbell's ... ready to serve	100g	88	21
Maggi ... recons. with water	100g	35	8
fish ... Campbell's ... ready to serve	100g	14	3
vegetable ... Campbell's ... ready to serve	100g	63	15
stock cubes ... 1 cube + 250ml water	5g	20	5
stout ... av all brands	100g	165	39
Carbine	100g	189	45
Guinness	100g	235	56
Swan/CUB Sheaf	100g	216	52
Strasbourg see *luncheon meat*			
strawberries ... canned ... sweetened	100g	245	59
unsweetened	100g	90	22
fresh ... 1 cup whole berries	145g	120	29
frozen ... whole ... sweetened	100g	475	114
John West ... in syrup	100g	325	78
string beans see *beans, green*			
stuffing ... sage and onion	100g	960	229
savoury ... bread-based	100g	785	188
stuffing mix ... Tandaco ... seasoned	100g	1520	363
suet	100g	3560	851
suet mix ... Tandaco	100g	2370	566
sugar ... brown/raw/refined	5g	80	19
sugar cane ... juice	100g	305	73
stem	100g	250	60
sugar peas see *peas, snow/sugar*			
sugar substitutes ... equal ... 1 sachet ... 2 tsp	15		4
equal/sugarella/hermesetas ... 1 tablet	1.5		0
saccharin/cyclamate ... 1 tablet/1 drop	0		0
sugarine ... 4 drops	0		0
½ tablet	0		0

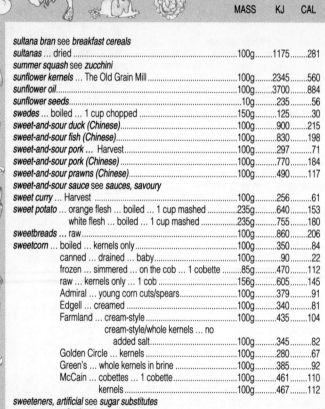

	MASS	KJ	CAL
sultana bran see *breakfast cereals*			
sultanas ... dried	100g	1175	281
summer squash see *zucchini*			
sunflower kernels ... The Old Grain Mill	100g	2345	560
sunflower oil	100g	3700	884
sunflower seeds	10g	235	56
swedes ... boiled ... 1 cup chopped	150g	125	30
sweet-and-sour duck (Chinese)	100g	900	215
sweet-and-sour fish (Chinese)	100g	830	198
sweet-and-sour pork ... Harvest	100g	297	71
sweet-and-sour pork (Chinese)	100g	770	184
sweet-and-sour prawns (Chinese)	100g	490	117
sweet-and-sour sauce see *sauces, savoury*			
sweet curry ... Harvest	100g	256	61
sweet potato ... orange flesh ... boiled ... 1 cup mashed	235g	640	153
white flesh ... boiled ... 1 cup mashed	235g	755	180
sweetbreads ... raw	100g	860	206
sweetcorn ... boiled ... kernels only	100g	350	84
canned ... drained ... baby	100g	90	22
frozen ... simmered ... on the cob ... 1 cobette	85g	470	112
raw ... kernels only ... 1 cob	156g	605	145
Admiral ... young corn cuts/spears	100g	379	91
Edgell ... creamed	100g	340	81
Farmland ... cream-style	100g	435	104
cream-style/whole kernels ... no added salt	100g	345	82
Golden Circle ... kernels	100g	280	67
Green's ... whole kernels in brine	100g	385	92
McCain ... cobettes ... 1 cobette	100g	461	110
kernels	100g	467	112
sweeteners, artificial see *sugar substitutes*			
sweets see *confectionery*			

	MASS	KJ	CAL

swiss roll see *cakes and pastries*

syrup, golden ....100g........1225........293

tabouli see *salads*

taco ....100g........905........216

taco salad ....100g........590........141

             with chilli con carne ....100g........465........111

tahini ... raw/roasted kernels ... 1 tbsp ....20g..........500........120

take-away foods see *Hungry Jack's*; *Kentucky Fried Chicken*;
   McDonald's; *Pizza Hut*

tamarillo ... raw ... flesh + seeds ... 1 av ....71g..........80..........19

tamarinds ... raw ....100g........1000........239

tangelo ... raw ... flesh only ... 1 av ....115g........180........43

tangerine see *mandarins*

tangor ....100g........145........35

taramasalata (Greek) see *dips and spreads*

taro ... boiled ... 1 cup sliced ....145g........640........153

tea ... black ... 1 cup ....250ml........5..........1

      black + 1 sugar ....250ml........85..........20

      white ... REV..250ml........70..........17

           whole milk...250ml........90..........22

      white + 1 sugar ... REV....................................250ml........150........36

               whole milk.........................250ml........170........41

tea, Indian ... without milk or sugar ....250ml........5..........1

	MASS	KJ	CAL
tempeh	100g	835	200
tofu ... canned ... fried	100g	1265	302
fresh	100g	380	91
steamed	100g	290	69
stirfried	100g	625	149
tomato juice see *fruit juices*			
tomato paste ... IXL ... no added salt	20g	60	14
Leggo's ... salt-free	20g	84	20
tomato puree ... av all brands	100g	145	35
tomato sauce see *sauces, savoury*			
tomato supreme ... Edgell	100g	210	50
tomatoes ... fried	100g	290	69
raw ... 1 av	129g	70	17
Admiral ... whole peeled ... in natural juice	100g	77	18
Edgell ... whole peeled	100g	67	16
SPC ... sliced tomatoes Italian/			
tomato onion capellery	100g	108	26
tomatoes, cherry ... raw ... 5	74g	40	10
tomatoes, egg ... raw ... 1 av	75g	45	11
tomatoes, stuffed (Greek)	100g	460	110
tommy ruff see *ruff, tommy/orange*			
tongue see *beef; lamb*			

Smoked Trout Pâté

75 g dill pickles
200 g smoked trout. skin and bones
   removed

275 g tofu, crumbled
2 tablespoons cider vinegar
1 level teaspoon French mustard

Drain dill pickles on paper towel and chop. Roughly flake the trout flesh and mix in a blender with tofu, vinegar and mustard until smooth. Stir in the chopped dill pickles. Divide between eight small containers. Label and freeze. Thaw at room temperature for 3 hours when required.

	MASS	KJ	CAL

toppings see *sauces, sweet*

tortellini Bolognese ... Heinz ... supersnack .... 100g ... 325 78

treacle ... 1 tbsp .... 22g ... 242 58

trevally ... fried .... 100g ... 845 202

        raw .... 100g ... 475 114

tripe ... cooked ... with parsley sauce .... 100g ... 420 100

        raw .... 100g ... 250 60

        stewed .... 100g ... 420 100

trout ... brook ... raw .... 100g ... 425 102

        brown ... steamed .... 100g ... 565 135

                   inc bones .... 100g ... 375 90

        lake .... 100g ... 1010 241

        rainbow ... raw .... 100g ... 815 195

tuna ... canned ... in brine ... drained ... 1 cup .... 190g ... 985 235

               in oil ... drained ... 1 cup .... 205g ... 1890 452

               sandwich type ... in oil ... 2 tbsp .... 40g ... 420 100

        raw .... 100g ... 1010 241

        Admiral ... toppers ... in matsaman curry .... 100g ... 598 143

        John West ... in brine/springwater ... drained .... 100g ... 480 115

               in canola oil ... drained .... 100g ... 866 207

        Weight Watchers ... in springwater .... 100g ... 325 78

tuna lasagne ... Findus Lean Cuisine ... 1 sv .... 275g ... 1130 270

turkey ... roasted .... 100g ... 1145 274

        Plumrose ... deli ... canned .... 100g ... 580 139

        Tegel ... flavour-basted ... breast/buffe .... 100g ... 625 149

               thigh .... 100g ... 500 120

               hindquarter ... flavour-basted ... uncooked ...... 100g ... 702 168

               smoked buffe ... cooked + skin .... 100g ... 550 131

turkey breast with tagliatelle ... Findus Lean Cuisine ... 1 sv ...... 240g ... 1110 265

turkey dijon ... Findus Lean Cuisine ... 1 sv .... 270g ... 1180 282

turkish delight see *confectionery*

turnip, white ... boiled ... 1 cup diced .... 240g ... 105 25

	MASS	KJ	CAL
turtle ... raw ... flesh only	100g	470	112
two fruits ... SPC ... in syrup	100g	230	55
lite	100g	180	43
nutradiet ... artific. sweet.	100g	105	25
snak pak ... in juice	140g	280	67
in syrup	140g	314	75
lite	140g	250	60
Weight Watchers ... artific. sweet.	100g	130	31
tyropita (Greek)	100g	1550	369
tzatziki (Greek) see *dips and spreads*			
veal			
boneless, average cut ... cooked ... lean ... 1 cup diced	190g	1185	283
lean + fat ... 1 cup diced	173g	1155	276
brains ... boiled	100g	450	108
crumbed, fried	100g	1220	292
cutlets ... crumbed, fried	140g	1265	302
forequarter ... simmered ... lean ... 1 cup diced	148g	1075	257
lean + fat ... 1 cup diced	158g	1235	295
leg ... baked ... lean ... 1 slice	44g	255	61
lean + fat ... 1 slice	45g	270	65
leg steak ... fried ... lean ... 1 av	65g	420	100

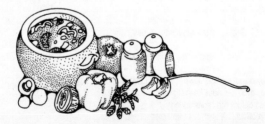

	MASS	KJ	CAL
lean+fat ... 1 av	67g	450	108
liver ... grilled ... 1 slice	85g	670	160
loin chop ... grilled ... lean ... 1 av	51g	310	74
lean+fat ... 1 av	54g	365	87
shank ... simmered ... lean ... 3 slices	80g	490	117
lean+fat ... 3 slices	90g	670	160
shoulder steak ... grilled ... lean ... 1 av	51g	310	74
lean+fat ... 1 av	53g	345	82
veal casserole ... with vegetables	100g	500	120
without vegetables	100g	590	141
veal schnitzel ... frozen ... fried ... av all brands	100g	1425	341
Baron's Table ... 1 sv	150g	1565	374
vegekabana ... tempeh ... 1 slice	16g	155	37
vegemite see *dips and spreads*			
vegetable and sausage ... Harvest	100g	265	63
vegetable and steak ... Harvest	100g	240	57
vegetable bakes ... Birds Eye ... 1 portion	94g	668	160
vegetable beef casserole	100g	465	111
vegetable curry	100g	755	180
vegetable fingers ... Birds Eye ... 1 piece	30g	230	55
vegetable juice ... canned	100ml	75	18
Campbell's ... V8	100ml	85	20
vegetable see individual vegetables			
vegetable salad, sweet-and-sour ... Always Fresh	100g	276	66
vegetables and noodles ... Dewcrisp ... easy serve	100g	360	86
vegetables and sausages ... Farmland	100g	425	102
Harvest	100g	258	62
Kraft	100g	390	93
vegetables and steak ... Farmland	150g	470	112
Harvest	100g	232	55
vegetables in sauce ... Birds Eye ... in cheese sauce	100g	362	87
in curry sauce	100g	229	55

	MASS	KJ	CAL
in herb sauce	100g	127	30
in satay sauce	100g	259	62
in S'n'S sauce	100g	193	46
in Thai sauce	100g	202	48
vegetables, mixed ... Edgell	100g	185	44
McCain	50g	79	19
Florentine	100g	218	52
Mediterranean	100g	154	37
Normandie	100g	262	63
vegetables steak and kidney ... Heinz ... supersnack	100g	475	114
venison ... roasted	100g	830	198
vermicelli ... dry ... uncooked	100g	1540	368
vine leaves	100g	65	16
stuffed	100g	455	109
vegetarian	100g	715	171
vinegar ... brown/red/white	100ml	50	12
cider	100ml	60	14
Cornwell's ... white/salt/cider/wine/spiced	100ml	60	14
vita brits see *breakfast cereals: Uncle Toby's*			
vodka see *spirits*			
vol-au-vent ... case without filling	100g	2400	574
waffles ... 1	60g	600	143
Nanna's ... 1	17g	192	46
walnuts ... shelled ... chopped ... 1 tbsp	12g	320	76
snack size	50g	1340	320
water buffalo ... feral	100g	645	154

Although salads usually contain little fat, the addition of oily dressings or mayonnaise can increase their fat content considerably. A low-fat, yoghurt-based dressing can help keep the kilojoule count down.

	MASS	KJ	CAL
water chestnuts ... canned ... drained solids	100g	205	49
Admiral	100g	230	55
watercress ... raw ... ¼ cup chopped	8g	5	1
watermelon see *melon*			
wax gourd see *gourd, wax*			
wax jambu ... raw ... 1 av	45g	40	10
weet-bix see *breakfast cereals*			
weeties see *breakfast cereals*			
Welsh rarebit	100g	1525	364
wheat starch	100g	1455	348
wheatgerm see *breakfast cereals*			
whisky see *spirits*			
whitebait ... fried	100g	2175	520
whiting, King George ... battered, deep-fried	100g	1315	314
floured, pan-fried	100g	635	152
steamed	100g	435	104
wines ... chablis/champagne ... 1 sv	120ml	420	100
dry red/dry white/rosé ... 1 sv	120ml	354	85
red ... 1 sv	120ml	432	103
sauterne ... 1 sv	120ml	450	108
sweet ... red ... 1 sv	120ml	606	145
white ... 1 sv	120ml	504	120
white chardonnay/semillon/riesling ... 1 sv	120ml	426	102
Seppelt ... reduced-alcohol ... chardonnay/ rhine riesling ... 1 sv	120ml	190	45
wines, fortified ... port	50ml	328	78
sherry ... dry	50ml	233	56
sweet	50ml	305	73
witloof see *chicory*			
yeast ... dried ... bakers	100g	1270	304
brewers	100g	1210	289

	MASS	KJ	CAL
fresh compressed ... bakers	100g	360	86
Fermipan ... dried ... granulated	100g	962	230
Tandaco ... dried	100g	1270	304
Winn ... lite yeast mix	100g	1600	382
wholemeal yeast mix	100g	1630	390

yoghurt

	MASS	KJ	CAL
fruit	100g	370	88
low-fat	100g	315	75
natural	100g	360	86
low-fat	100g	250	60
Bulla ... drinking yoghurt	100g	345	82
reduced-fat fruit	100g	399	95
reduced-fat plain	100g	328	78
soft-serve	100g	594	142
Dairy Farmers ... traditional low-fat natural	100g	210	50
traditional natural	100g	320	76
Danone ... danino ... reduced-fat fruit ... av all flavours	100g	380	91
vanilla	100g	398	95
diet-lite ... av all flavours	100g	192	46
fruit ... av all flavours	100g	391	93
light and fruity	100g	302	72
Fruche ... av all flavours	100g	496	119
Jalna ... honey	100g	300	72
leben/mild continental	100g	280	67
premium blend/bio-dynamic	100g	406	97
skim-milk ... plain	100g	217	52
skim-milk/tropical/berry fruits	100g	360	86
vanilla	100g	250	60
Oak ... frozen	100g	630	151
fruit	100g	425	102
plain	100g	390	93
Pauls ... extra fruit ... av all flavours	100g	389	93

	MASS	KJ	CAL
low-fat ... plain	100g	203	49
natural set	100g	349	83
natural set low-fat	100g	244	58
Trim low fat ... av all flavours	100g	292	70
Ski ... apricot	100g	400	96
av all other flavours	100g	405	97
Ski lite ... berries and cherries	100g	355	85
av all other flavours	100g	325	78
Weight Watchers ... fruit salad/strawberry	100g	148	35
natural	100g	205	49
Yofresh ... apple and vanilla/black cherry	100g	445	106
fruit of paradise	100g	438	105
Greek style	100g	651	156
natural	100g	304	73
peach mango	100g	449	107
Yofresh low-fat ... apricot/strawberry	100g	340	81
peach melba/vanilla	100g	385	92
Yogo ... banana/strawb/spearmint	100g	434	104
chocolate/chocolate caramel	100g	447	107
tropical banana/chocolate cherry	100g	415	99
Yomix ... fruit ... av all flavours	100g	357	85
natural	100g	223	53
vanilla	100g	320	76
Yoplait ... apricot/strawb/fruit tango/redberry cocktail ... pack	200g	765	183
banana and passionpeach/orchard fruit/ tropical fruit/fruit of the forest/fruit salad ... pack	200g	795	190
kiwifruit and mango/peach and guava ... pack	200g	785	188
pineapple and mandarin ... pack	200g	740	177
Yoplait low-fat ... blueberry/strawb and guava ... pack	200g	705	168
fruit salad/peach and cherry/strawb and peach/tropical fruit ... pack	200g	720	172
strawb/strawb and banana/apricot ... pack	200g	685	164

	MASS	KJ	CAL
Yorkshire pudding	100g	900	215
youngberries ... fresh ... raw	100g	245	59
zucchini ... average type ... boiled ... 1 cup sliced	155g	100	24
raw ... 1 cup sliced	130g	75	18
golden ... boiled ... 1 cup sliced	155g	120	29
raw ... slices	60g	40	10
green-skinned ... boiled ... 1 cup sliced	155g	95	23
raw ... 1 av	84g	50	12
zucchini lasagne ... Findus Lean Cuisine ... 1 sv	310g	1090	261
zucchini, stuffed (Lebanese)	100g	535	128

INTRODUCTION TO THE TABLE

Five food components — fat, cholesterol, sodium, calcium and dietary fibre — have important implications for our health, either because we may be eating too much of them (in the case of fat, cholesterol and sodium) or because we may not be eating enough (in the case of calcium and dietary fibre).

This section of *The Australian Calorie Counter* explains how each component affects health and suggests practical ways of keeping your intake at a desirable level. To find specific information about the amounts of the five components in a wide range of foods, consult the Table (pp. 187–217).

FAT

For most people, the type of fat eaten is characteristic of their culture, for example butter in Northern Europe, olive oil in Mediterranean countries and soya bean and sesame seed oils in Asia. The fat obtained from animals and dairy products is also characteristic of different cultures.

The purpose of fat
Whatever the source, dietary fats generally serve the same purpose: they add flavour and texture to food and supply energy and essential nutrients, including fat-soluble vitamins A, D, E and K, and the fatty acids needed by the body.

The three main types

The fats in our diet have different compositions depending on the types of fatty acids they contain. There are three main types of fatty acids: **saturated**, **mono-unsaturated** and **polyunsaturated**. All fats contain a mixture of these but the predominance of one type gives the fat its main characteristics.

In general, most saturated fats, for example butter, meat fat, copha and solid cooking fats, are solid at room temperature. Mono-unsaturated fats, for example olive oil and canola oil, are usually liquid at room temperature. Polyunsaturated fats, for example the vegetable, seed and nut oils (sunflower, peanut and safflower), are also normally liquid at room temperature.

Polyunsaturated margarines are made from vegetable oils that have been processed to give them a spreading consistency. The lower-fat dairy spreads and margarines are processed to incorporate a higher water content.

The oils in fish contain a special class of polyunsaturated omega-3 fatty acids, which some researchers suggest may protect against coronary heart disease. These substances are highest in darker fish such as salmon, tuna, sardines and herrings.

Fat and health

The amount and type of fat in our diet receives a great deal of attention. Research shows that a high-fat diet, particularly a diet high in saturated fats, can increase blood cholesterol and increase the risk of heart disease, stroke and some cancers.

For these reasons health authorities recommend that we reduce the total fat in our diet to 30 per cent of the daily energy intake (measured in kilojoules or calories). At present the average Australian diet contains about 34 per cent energy from fat. In effect this means that we should eat not more than 9 grams of fat for every

1000 kilojoules (240 calories) of energy. (*Note*: This restriction does not apply to children under five.)

A further recommendation is that not more than one-third of the fat eaten should come from saturated fats: accordingly, you should replace saturated fats with mono-unsaturated and polyunsaturated fats wherever possible.

The most important step is to cut down the total amount of fat and foods that contain fat. This is an efficient way of reducing energy intake because fat is the most concentrated source of energy in our diet, supplying 37 kilojoules (9 calories) per gram.

How to reduce your fat intake
Eat more of the following non-fat or low-fat foods:

■ fruit, vegetables and legumes (dried peas, beans, lentils and chick peas)
■ pasta and cereals, including cereals such as rice, cracked wheat, barley and corn, and wholegrain breakfast cereals
■ wholemeal bread, flat bread and crispbread
■ low-fat milk and yoghurt, reduced-fat tasty and processed cheese, cottage and ricotta cheese
■ fish, fat-trimmed meat and skinless chicken.

Limit the following:

■ butter and margarine (to 20 grams per day), cream, sour cream, full-fat cheeses and standard ice-cream
■ croissants, cream buns, doughnuts, pastries, chocolate and cream cakes, and biscuits
■ chocolate, chocolate bars, carob bars, caramels and fudge
■ avocados, olives and nuts
■ fat-basted and fried, crumbed and battered foods – including oven-baked crumbed and battered convenience foods

■ soups and sauces made with roux, cream, butter, eggs or cheese
■ high-fat snack foods, including potato crisps
■ the hidden-fat foods – traditional mayonnaises and dressings, certain 'dry' biscuits, frozen and packaged convenience meals, packet cake and pudding mixes, take-away foods, and toasted muesli.

Practise some cunning dodges:

buy lean cuts, and trim fat from meat, skin from poultry
skim all fat from casseroles, cooked mince, soup stock and gravy juices
use a non-stick frying pan, and a rack for roasting
steam or microwave vegetables rather than frying them
■ use purees of fruit or vegetables as sauces
spread butter or margarine thinly, and omit it when you are using moist sandwich fillings
■ choose low-fat alternatives in the supermarket – light salad dressings, reduced-fat spreads
look for the National Heart Foundation tick on brand items when you shop
look for low-fat take-away and convenience foods.

CHOLESTEROL

Cholesterol is a fatty substance not present in plant foods but found in all animal tissue (including human tissue), where it is essential to life and present in all body cells. It carries out many important functions and is produced by the liver as it is needed, regardless of whether cholesterol is consumed in the diet.

Blood cholesterol

Blood carries cholesterol to any part of the body that requires it, but if the level of blood cholesterol is too high it is likely that deposits of cholesterol will form on the lining of arteries, causing them to narrow and harden. This condition is known as atherosclerosis. If atherosclerosis becomes severe the arteries can become blocked by small blood clots. A heart attack can occur if the blockage is in a blood vessel of the heart.

There are different types of cholesterol in the blood and, although there are special methods to measure them separately, it is usual to measure total blood cholesterol. The National Heart Foundation recommends that the total blood-cholesterol level for Australians should be not more than 5.5 mmol/L (millimoles per litre). Your doctor can arrange for you to have your level checked. Many Australians have high levels (6.5 mmol/L or more), increasing their risk of coronary heart disease.

What determines blood-cholesterol level?

The amount of cholesterol in the blood depends on several factors, including hereditary influences, overweight, exercise, smoking and diet. Of these factors, we have some control over all but the first. If high blood cholesterol is a characteristic of your family it is important to have regular checks and to keep to the recommended lifestyle and dietary guidelines.

The most important dietary factors implicated in raised blood-cholesterol levels are:

■ high-fat diets
diets high in saturated fats
diets in which the proportion of saturated fat is high in comparison to mono-unsaturated and polyunsaturated fats.

Other dietary factors related to high blood-cholesterol levels are:

■ a high intake of cholesterol from food
a low intake of dietary fibre.

Control your blood cholesterol with the following measures:

aim for the healthy weight range (see 'Health and eating habits', p. 4)
reduce total intake of fat and oil, and of saturated fats (see 'Fat', p. 169)
include some mono-unsaturated and polyunsaturated fat in your daily fat intake
limit cholesterol intake from food sources (not more than 300 milligrams of cholesterol per day)
■ increase foods high in dietary fibre (see 'Dietary Fibre', p. 182)
■ keep to a regular exercise and activity programme
avoid smoking
■ avoid excess alcohol.

SODIUM

The sodium we eat comes mainly from the chemical compound we call **salt** (sodium chloride), although it is also found in other chemical compounds in our food (for example bicarbonate of soda and monosodium glutamate [msg]) and also occurs naturally in some fresh foods (for example meat and vegetables). In the Table (see pp. 187–217) figures are given for the sodium content of food; in most cases, but not all, that sodium is part of the salt that has been added to food in cooking and processing.

Why cut down on salt?
The Australian Dietary Guidelines advise using less salt as a practical way of keeping sodium intake down to a healthy level.

Our 'Western' diet has conditioned us to like salt added to our food; but research indicates that for some people a high intake of sodium can lead to high blood pressure, and it has been shown that where the overall salt intake is high a larger proportion of the population has higher-than-normal blood pressure. On the other hand, among communities eating only naturally occurring sodium (for example Australian Aborigines eating traditional food) there is no increase in blood pressure with advancing age as there commonly is in communities eating a 'Western' diet.

How much salt?
For most people there is enough naturally occurring sodium in a varied diet. The average person's requirement is 230 milligrams per day – the amount of sodium in about one-tenth of a teaspoon of salt (one teaspoon [6 grams] of salt contains 2.3 grams of sodium).

The average Australian consumes one-and-a-half to two teaspoons of salt per day (9–12 grams of salt or 3.5–4.6 grams of sodium). Government health recommendations, which work towards ideal targets from the starting point of what people are actually eating, advise that we reduce our daily intake to between half and one teaspoon (3–6 grams) of salt (1.2 – 2.3 grams of sodium).

Salt regulation in the body

Most sodium in the human body occurs as sodium chloride, or salt. The body, particularly by means of the kidneys, has a marvellous capacity to regulate its water and salt levels. Even during hot weather, when people perspire more, there is no need for most to take extra salt because the body conserves salt if it is needed. It is much more important to replace the water lost through perspiration.

Salt in our food

Our dietary habits provide us with four main ways of taking in sodium:

- through sodium naturally present in fresh foods
- through salt added to many processed foods
- in salt added during the cooking
- in salt added at the table.

About half our daily intake of sodium comes from the salt in processed foods, some of them basic items of the daily diet, for example bread, butter, margarine, cheese and processed breakfast cereals.

Your excess sodium may come from the salt used in preserving processes, as in the case of corned beef, ham, bacon, salami, smoked cod, smoked salmon, caviar, anchovies, olives and vegemite; from salty sauces and seasonings, for example soy sauce, fish sauce, and stock cubes; or from salt added more directly for flavour, as in the case of many take-away foods, including hamburgers, chips and crisps, salted nuts, and other snack foods.

Then there are the hidden-sodium foods – sweet biscuits, breakfast cereals, cakes and pastries. In addition, there is sodium in soda water, fizzy drinks taken for indigestion, and some common painkillers. Consult your doctor if you are concerned about the sodium levels in any drugs you take regularly.

A brief guide to sodium levels in foods

The following information refers to standard foods rather than to low-salt versions.

Highest in sodium (more than 2.5 g/100 g) are:

■ all types of salt including table salt, cooking salt, rock salt, sea salt, and vegetable salts such as celery salt and garlic salt
■ stock cubes, gravy powders, soy sauce, fish sauce, msg, seasoning powders, yeast and vegetable extracts (vegemite and marmite), anchovies, and anchovy paste.

Foods high in sodium (1.0 – 2.5 g/100 g) include:

■ commercial and home-made bottled sauces and pickles, gherkins and olives, French dressing, prepared mustard
■ ham, bacon, corned beef, salami, luncheon meats, frankfurts, sausages and pâté
■ salted snack foods – pretzels, twisties, crisps, cracker biscuits
■ parmesan, processed cheddar, fetta, haloumy and pepato cheeses
■ take-away foods – meat pies, sausage rolls, pizza, hamburgers and Chinese food
■ standard butter and margarine
■ packet soups
■ canned sardines, salmon and tuna, and smoked salmon, caviar, and fish paste.

Foods moderately high in sodium (0.3 – 1.0 g/100 g) include:

■ potato chips and salted nuts
  sweet biscuits, cakes and pastries
  canned vegetables and vegetable juice
■ some breakfast cereals, including toasted muesli
■ canned soups
  toffees.

Foods low in sodium (less than 0.3 g/100 g) include:

  fresh and frozen fruits and vegetables
  fresh meat, poultry, fish and eggs
  most beverages, including fruit juice, milk, beer, wine and many
  soft drinks
■ cereals and pasta cooked without salt, plain white and wholemeal flour, dried beans and lentils, unsalted seeds and nuts
■ untoasted muesli, puffed wheat and rice, unprocessed bran
■ quark, cottage and ricotta cheese
  sugar, jam, honey, plain boiled sweets, jelly beans and
  peppermints
  herbs, spices and oils.

Reducing your intake

To meet the Dietary Guidelines and the demand created by an increasingly health-conscious public, some companies produce low-salt or salt-reduced versions of standard products, for example low-salt butter, margarine, cheese, or canned soup. Choose low-salt versions for preference; however, remember that a low-salt food may not be appropriate in other ways, perhaps by having a high fat or high sugar content: so use your judgement.

It can take up to three months to adjust to a lower salt taste. It is best if babies and young children don't acquire the taste for salty foods in the first place. For many people, adding salt to food is a habit. Good advice is to:

- taste food before adding salt
- use a salt shaker with smaller holes, or better still put it away
- gradually reduce the amount of salt used in cooking
- try different herbs and spices in cooking to give extra flavour and variety
- don't add salt to dessert, cake, pastry and biscuit recipes
- refrigerate fetta cheese in water
- bring corned beef or smoked cod to the boil in water, and discard the water before proceeding with the usual cooking process
- limit the quantity of salty foods eaten
- read the labels, and choose reduced-salt or salt-free varieties of processed foods as often as possible.

CALCIUM

Calcium has important functions in the body, the most easily recognised being its role in bone formation. More than 99 per cent of the calcium in the body is present in the bones. It is well known that babies and children need the calcium in milk and milk products to develop strong, healthy bones and teeth.

Calcium is essential in several other body processes, including blood clotting, nerve transmission, muscle contraction and some enzyme actions.

Your calcium intake
Your intake of calcium should come from foods – calcium supplements should be taken only on medical advice.

The following table gives the recommended intakes for children and adults.

Recommended dietary intakes of calcium
(mg/day)

Subject	Age	Recommended intake
Infants	0–6 months (breast milk)	300
	0–6 months (cow's milk)	500
	7–12 months	550
Children	1–3 years	700
(both sexes)	4–7 years	800
Girls	8–11 years	900
	12–15 years	1000
	16–18 years	800
Boys	8–11 years	800
	12–15 years	1200
	16–18 years	1000
Women	19–50* years	800
	After menopause	1000
	Pregnant	+300**
	Lactating	+400
Men	19–65+ years	800

*   Menopause
** Third trimester

Taken from: Nordin, B.E.C. Ch. 17, 'Calcium', in Recommended Nutrient Intakes: Australian Papers. A.S. Truswell (ed.), Australian Professional Publications, 1990, p.213.

Osteoporosis

Like other body tissues, bone is continually being broken down and rebuilt, so throughout life a daily intake of calcium in food is needed for the rebuilding process. With increasing age this rebuilding process slows down: in the elderly more calcium may be lost from bone than is re-absorbed, causing the bones to become weaker and more porous, a condition known as osteoporosis. Bone-thinning is a normal condition of ageing occurring in both men and women; however, it occurs more rapidly in women following menopause when levels of the hormone oestrogen are reduced.

There are three main factors associated with the development of osteoporosis.

1   Genetic characteristics influence bone strength – small-boned, white Caucasian women are the most susceptible to osteoporosis.
2   Exercise is a major factor. Lack of exercise increases bone loss, for example in the bedridden; conversely, women can suffer bone loss if they exercise so much that their hormone levels drop to the point where menstruation is delayed or ceases (a situation similar to menopause). This can occur in ballet dancers and athletes.
3   Heavy drinkers and smokers increase their risk of calcium loss.

Note: Bone calcium loss can also occur in people suffering from the 'dieting disease' anorexia nervosa, particularly in women if the condition results in the cessation of menstruation, which is linked with lower production of oestrogen.

Guarding against osteoporosis

In particular, girls and young women should build up their bone stores of calcium so that they can withstand the natural depletion in middle and old age. The following are general recommendations.

- Keep up the recommended calcium intake.
- Develop the habit of moderate, regular, weight-bearing exercise. Walking, jogging, tennis, golf and dancing are all suitable. While swimming has many benefits it doesn't qualify as a weight-bearing exercise.
- Limit alcohol consumption.
- Avoid smoking.
- Limit caffeine consumption.
- Use less salt.

Useful dietary sources of calcium

The best dietary sources of calcium are milk, cheese and yoghurt. For adults, low-fat milk and milk products are recommended as these do not supply excess kilojoules, fat or cholesterol.

Other useful dietary sources are certain green vegetables, including broccoli and haricot beans; certain nuts, for example almonds; dried fruits, for example figs; and fish with edible bones, for example sardines and salmon. Soy drinks used as milk substitutes provide some calcium; certain brands add extra calcium to make the drink more like milk in the nutrients it supplies, so check the labels.

DIETARY FIBRE

In the days of our grandparents dietary fibre was described as roughage, the indigestible part of food – a waste product of no nutritional value. It is now recognised as a most important constituent of our diet, essential for good health. Dietary fibre helps to relieve constipation, fight bowel and breast cancer, lower cholesterol levels and improve control of diabetes.

There are two main types: insoluble fibre and soluble fibre. Each serves a different function in the body and is found in different plant foods. Animal foods, meat and dairy products do not contain dietary fibre.

Insoluble fibre

Cereal foods, particularly in the bran portion of wheat and rice, are the main sources of insoluble fibre. It is present in wheat bran; wholegrain breakfast cereals made from wheat; wholemeal and mixed-grain breads; cakes, biscuits and muffins made from wholemeal flour; wholemeal pasta products; brown rice; rice bran; and vegetables belonging to the cabbage family.

These insoluble fibres help in the prevention and relief of constipation. Fibre absorbs water in the bowel and in the process softer, bulkier stools are formed. In the longer term this can help prevent bowel diseases such as diverticulitis, haemorrhoids and cancer.

Soluble fibre

This type of fibre is found particularly in rolled oats and oat bran; barley and barley bran; and brown rice and rice bran (which contain insoluble fibre as well); legumes such as beans, lentils and chick peas; and vegetables and fruit (which also contain insoluble fibre).

Soluble fibre has little laxative effect but is valuable in helping to reduce blood-cholesterol levels.

Fibre in the diet

Foods high in dietary fibre – fruit, vegetables, legumes and wholegrain breads and cereals – are generally low in fat. (The main exception is nuts.) Most of these foods are bulky, giving a feeling of fullness and satisfying the appetite without supplying excess calories, so making them useful in weight control. Because they are digested more slowly than refined foods they are also recommended in diabetics' diets.

Health authorities recommend an intake of 25–30 grams of fibre per day from a variety of sources to ensure the benefits of different types. Eating large amounts of one type of fibre (for example wheat bran or a fibre supplement) is not recommended.

To make the most of fibre foods consumed it is important to drink plenty of fluid. If your fibre intake has been low it is advisable to increase it gradually to avoid possible bowel discomfort.

How to increase your dietary fibre

Eat more of the following:

- fruit and vegetables – fresh, dried, frozen and canned. Use raw and unpeeled fruit and vegetables whenever possible.
- legumes – baked beans, bean-mix salads, homous and casseroles (for example chilli con carne), and lentils, kidney beans and chick peas added to soups (for example minestrone and split-pea)
- wholemeal breads, wholegrain and bran breakfast cereals, wholemeal pasta and brown rice.

Add nuts and seeds to increase variety – in sandwiches, salads and snacks.

The chart on p. 185 shows you how to make changes to your menu to include more dietary fibre and less fat.

Choose this ...	**... instead of this**
fresh or stewed fruit	fruit juice, flavoured milk
wholegrain cereal, natural muesli	rice bubbles, fruit loops
wholemeal toast	white toast
marmalade	butter, honey
dried fruit, wholemeal muffin	potato crisps, doughnut
wholemeal salad roll (with tuna, lean roast beef or skinless chicken pieces)	meat pie, pastie
crispbread with low-fat cheese	crackers with cheddar cheese
new potatoes in jackets	peeled or mashed potatoes
steamed or microwaved vegetables, brown rice	fried chips
stir-fried vegetables (minimum oil)	vegetables with a knob of butter
wholemeal dinner roll	garlic bread
fruit salad with low-fat yoghurt	cheesecake, apple pie, steamed pudding with custard

THE
TABLE

*Values are given for 100g unless specified otherwise.	FAT g/ 100g+	CHOL mg/ 100g+	SOD mg/ 100g+	CALC mg/ 100g+	FIBRE* g/ 100g+
Biscuits					
anzac	24	18	230	61	3.6
carob	30	7	160	140	1.4
choc-coated/chip ... av type	24	14	300	60	1.4
crackers ... cheese	22	14	960	120	3.4
rye crispbreads	2.5	tr**	480	38	14
savoury shapes	24	8	1100	64	3.4
wholemeal + sesame	15.7	6	730	53	7
cream-filled	24	23	450	60	1.4
shortbread	25	29	480	35	1.9
sweet ... fruit-filled	10	3	150	40	2.8
iced	12.8	16	250	24	1.5
jam-filled	17.7	18	130	34	1.8
nut	27	31	440	90	1.9
plain	16	15	300	36	2
wafers ... cream-filled	28	19	110	52	
Arnotts ... Jatz	20.3		950		2.5
Salada ... av all varieties	9.4		890		3.6
Sao	15.9		660		3.2
Thin Captain	9.8		740		3.7
Vita Weat ... av all varieties	9		550		12.5
Water Cracker ... av all varieties	7.7		630		3.5
Players ... wafers ... av all varieties	22.3		55	48	
Breads					
bread ... brown	2.5	0	500	60	5
white	2.5	0	450	60	2.7

*Dietary fibre values are derived from figures based on the AOAC (Association of Official Analytical Chemists) method.

**The figure 0 indicates an absence of this nutrient in the food. A trace of the nutrient is indicated by the abbreviation 'tr'. No entry indicates that no figures are yet available.

*Values are given for 100g unless specified otherwise.	FAT g/ 100g+	CHOL mg/ 100g+	SOD mg/ 100g+	CALC mg/ 100g+	FIBRE* g/ 100g+
1 slice av white ... 28g	0.7	0	130	14	0.8
breadcrumbs ... dried	3.6	0	670	64	4.1
bread roll ... white	2.6	tr	700	60	3.1
wholemeal	2.4	tr	720	48	5.7
croissant ... 1 ... av type ... 65g	15.3	18	240	50	2.9
crumpet ... 2 ... av type ... 100g	0.7	tr	950	83	2.3
garlic bread	17.4	12	380	72	2.6
Lebanese/pita/flat ... white	2.3	0	520	20	2.8
wholemeal	2	0	450	20	6.3
mixed-grain	2.8	0	470	54	5
muffin ... English	1.4	tr	420	120	2.4
fruit	1.7	tr	470	110	2.5
raisin/fruit loaf	3.9	0	190	45	3
rye ... dark	1.8	0	510	73	7.1
light	2	0	510	39	4.5
white ... high-fibre	2.7	0	440	60	4.3
wholemeal	2.9	0	470	54	6.5

⁺Values are given for 100g unless specified otherwise.	FAT g/ 100g⁺	CHOL mg/ 100g⁺	SOD mg/ 100g⁺	CALC mg/ 100g⁺	FIBRE⁺ g/ 100g⁺
high-fibre	3.2	0	450	48	7.8
Buttercup ... wholemeal plus	2.2	0	445		7.2
wonder white	2.5	0	480		5.3
Ploughmans ... wholegrain	2.7	0	440		7.1
barley and oats	3.7	0	420		6.9
Tip Top ... mighty white	2.6	0	480	146	3.0
weight watchers	2.6	0	480	300	2.0
Vogel ... wholemeal and sesame	6.2	0	350		8.4

Breakfast Cereals

	FAT g/ 100g⁺	CHOL mg/ 100g⁺	SOD mg/ 100g⁺	CALC mg/ 100g⁺	FIBRE⁺ g/ 100g⁺
bran ... oat, raw	7	0	4	58	15.9
rice	20.4	0	8	58	25.5
wheat	4.5	0	18	87	44.7
cornflakes	1	0	1190	5	3.3
muesli ... non-toasted ... av	9.2	0	55	110	12.5
toasted ... av sample	16.6	0	170	65	8.7
oatmeal/rolled oats ... boiled ... no salt	1.1	0	1	8	1.3
rice bubbles	0.8	0	970	23	1
vita brits/weet-bix ... av sample	2.3	0	390	30	10.5
weeties	2.1	0	510	29	11
wheat, puffed	2.1	0	1	29	12.1
wheatgerm	7.8	0	240	41	41.7
Farmland ... no-added-salt toasted muesli	19		25		4
Kellogg's ... all-bran ... fruit'n oats	3.3	0	580		19.6
coco pops	0.3	0	736	30	1.3
cornflakes	1.3	0	933		3.3
komplete natural muesli	3		37		8.7
rice bubbles	3.3	0	1010		1
sustain	3	0	113		7.3

Watch out for any hidden fats in cakes, biscuits, snacks and convenience foods you buy. Choose 'light' and reduced-fat versions of foods traditionally high in fat.

*Values are given for 100g unless specified otherwise.	FAT g/ 100g+	CHOL mg/ 100g+	SOD mg/ 100g+	CALC mg/ 100g+	FIBRE* g/ 100g+
Uncle Toby's ... 1-min. oats/traditional oats	7.6	0	10	75	10
crunchy oatbran and fruit	4.3	0	280	50	13.8
instant porridge + honey	5.7	2	20	75	6.8
sportsplus	2.7	0	185	500	7.8

Butter, Margarines, Fats and Oils

	FAT	CHOL	SOD	CALC	FIBRE
butter ... salt-reduced ... av type	81.3	260	350	17	0
standard ... salted	81.3	260	843	17	0
10g ... 2 tsp	8.1	26	84	1.7	0
unsalted ... av type	81.3	260	8	17	0
Western Star ... light	59.7	180	350		
ghee	99	300	5	10	0
margarine ... cooking	81	105	840	18	0
polyunsaturated ... av type	81	0	833	20	0
reduced-fat ... av type	40	0	300	5	0
table ... av type	81	31	840	20	0
Meadow Lea ... salt-reduced	81	0	390	15	0
vegetable oils	99.7	0	tr	tr	0

Cakes, Pastries and Puddings

	FAT	CHOL	SOD	CALC	FIBRE
apple crumble	7.8		450	65	
apple pie	11.6	14	288	6	1.5
McDonald's	17.5	17	232	22	1.6
apple strudel	9.7	11	340	28	1.5
baklava	19.8	17	260	42	2
black forest cake	19.3	57	280	57	0.7
bun, fruit	8	4	200	100	3.3
carrot cake	17.7	54	330	50.	2.5
cheesecake	22.2	46	270	110	1
chocolate cake	17.9	105	500	77	1.5
chocolate eclair	25.9	97	160	48	0.5

+Values are given for 100g unless specified otherwise.	FAT g/ 100g+	CHOL mg/ 100g+	SOD mg/ 100g+	CALC mg/ 100g+	FIBRE* g/ 100g+
chocolate pudding, self-saucing	6.8	50	200	33	1
Christmas pudding	6.7	40	317	99	3
cupcake, plain, iced	14.9	54	370	4	1.1
custard	3	11	85	100	0
custard powder ... dry	0.7		320	15	0
custard tart	13.1	54	270	74	1
Danish pastry	15.5	35	40	45	2.3
date and nut loaf	11.5	30	375	64	3
doughnut	20.6	34	380	41	2.2
fruit cake ... boiled	9.7	37	392	40	2.9
light	13.9	52	360	43	3.3
dark	11.6	24	312	56	3.4
fruit mince slice	9.4	20	220	35	2.1
jam tart	14.9	16	200	13	0.9
jelly crystals	0	0	500	4	0
lamington	12	31	140	6	2.3
madeira cake ... home-made	17	91	550	70	1.6
meringue	1.4	0	40	3	0
muesli slice	23	29	300	45	3
pancakes, plain	15	45	90	100	1
pastry ... biscuit crust	23.4	7	405	80	1.9
filo ... raw	2.2	tr	800	18	1.4
puff ... baked	26.5	30	545	10	1.6
shortcrust ... baked	30	36	460	12	2
wholemeal ... baked	26.3	28	465	23	10.4
plum pudding ... canned	7	22	350	51	2.6
quiche	22	130	530	14	0.7
scones ... plain	8.2	10	620	138	1.7
sultana	9	11	310	100	3
sponge ... filled	14	130	240	46	0.9
plain	6	68	170	55	0.9
Swiss roll	7	36	250	26	1.5

+Values are given for 100g unless specified otherwise.	FAT g/ 100g+	CHOL mg/ 100g+	SOD mg/ 100g+	CALC mg/ 100g+	FIBRE* g/ 100g+
vanilla slice	8.9	8	170	70	0.4

Cereals

	FAT	CHOL	SOD	CALC	FIBRE
barley, pearl ... boiled	0.8	0	8	10	3.5
bulgur ... soaked	0.9	0	2	12	8
flour ... plain, white	1.2	0	2	20	3.8
self-raising, white	1.2	0	700	107	3.8
wholemeal	2.1	0	3	30	11.2
pasta ... white ... cooked ... no added salt	0.5	0	3	8	1.7
wholemeal	0.8	0	5	28	5.7
see also *Fish and Fish Foods; Meats; Take-away and Convenience Meals*					
rice ... white ... boiled ... with salt ... av salting	0.6	0	300	7	0.2
without salt	0.6	0	5	17	0.2
brown ... boiled	0.6	0	9	11	0.5
fried see *Take-away and Convenience Meals*					
rye flour	2.3	0	4	44	1.5
soya flour	20	0	2	210	21

Cheese and Cheese Foods

cheese ...	FAT	CHOL	SOD	CALC	FIBRE
blue vein	32.5	120	1000	540	0
brie	29.1	96	604	468	0
camembert	26.3	93	652	478	0

Nutty Blue Cheese Spread

75 g Danish blue cheese, crumbled
275 g low-fat cottage cheese

3 tablespoons skim milk
25 g walnuts, chopped

Blend blue cheese, cottage cheese and skim milk until smooth. Stir in walnuts. Divide between 6 small containers. Label and freeze. Thaw at room temperature for 3 hours, as needed. Makes 6 servings at 480 kJ (115 Cal) per portion.

*Values are given for 100g unless specified otherwise.	FAT g/100g⁺	CHOL mg/100g⁺	SOD mg/100g⁺	CALC mg/100g⁺	FIBRE* g/100g⁺
cheddar	33.8	102	647	779	0
cottage	9.3	36	200	67	0
cream	33	97	420	104	0
edam	27.9	88	676	848	0
fetta	23.3	75	1060	353	0
mozzarella	23.1	71	367	817	0
parmesan	31.5	101	1371	1091	0
processed	27.5	83	1350	625	0
reduced-salt and -fat	25	75	300	800	0
quark	9.6	32	100	85	0
quark/cottage ... low-fat ... av type	1.2	11	130	77	0
ricotta	11.3	48	200	223	0
Bega so-light ... reduced-fat	26	85	610	870	0
Gold'n Canola mild	22	20	730	900	0
Kraft light	17	52	1290	400	0
cheese souffle	16.9	450	590	236	tr
cheese spreads	27	75	1400	400	0

Confectionery

	FAT g/100g⁺	CHOL mg/100g⁺	SOD mg/100g⁺	CALC mg/100g⁺	FIBRE* g/100g⁺
caramels ... plain	11.1	14	226	138	tr
with nuts	16.3	13	203	140	5
carob drink powder	8.4				19
chocolate ... dark	30	tr	55	50	1
milk	28	18	90	250	0.8
toffee fudge ... av type	15	20	300	80	1.5
Allen's ... buttermenthols	0.3		343	7	
Irish moss	tr		68	4.5	

Eggs

	FAT g/100g⁺	CHOL mg/100g⁺	SOD mg/100g⁺	CALC mg/100g⁺	FIBRE* g/100g⁺
egg ... fried in oil ... 55g	21.3	201	51	25	0
poached ... 55g	5.3	180	41	24	0

*Values are given for 100g unless specified otherwise.	FAT g/100g*	CHOL mg/100g*	SOD mg/100g*	CALC mg/100g*	FIBRE* g/100g*
raw ... 55g	4.8	180	64	19	0
scrambled	15	500	145	90	0
egg omelette	13.1	410	145	52	0
egg white ... 31g	0	0	54	2	0
egg yolk ... 17g	4.8	180	10	17	0

Fish and Fish Foods

	FAT g/100g*	CHOL mg/100g*	SOD mg/100g*	CALC mg/100g*	FIBRE* g/100g*
anchovies, fillets ... canned	9	77	5500	170	0
anchovy paste	11.2	80	9604	14	0
bream ... steamed	5.4	85	80	25	0
calamari ... fried	10	200	320	14	0
caviar ... black	5.4	286	2120	10	0
red	8.2	350	1850	30	0
cod ... smoked ... simmered	1.5	60	550	31	0
crab ... canned	0.6	84	700	170	0
in black-bean sauce	10.1	56	720	120	0
eel ... smoked	28		100	20	0
fish ... deep-fried in batter ... av sample	12	70	200	24	0.4
floured, pan-fried in oil	10	75	130	40	tr
in batter ... frozen ... oven-fried	19.3	27	320	17	0.4
in white sauce	5	100	200	60	tr
steamed ... av sample	3	85	100	45	0
fish cakes ... deep-fried	14.6	20	980	160	0.7

*Values are given for 100g unless specified otherwise.	FAT g/100g+	CHOL mg/100g+	SOD mg/100g+	CALC mg/100g+	FIBRE* g/100g+
fish cocktail ... deep-fried	16.9	26	460	24	0.9
fish fingers ... frozen ... fried	16	26	300	33	0.9
grilled ... no added salt	11.3	31	80	35	0.4
fish paste ... canned	4.2	80	1400	280	0
flake ... in batter ... deep-fried	5.6	43	250	13	0.4
gemfish/mullet ... crumbed ... fried	18.5	70	120	16	0.4
herring fillets in tomato sauce	4.9		1580	100	tr
lobster	0.9	116	400	50	0
mussels ... smoked ... canned in oil	10.4	92	460	70	0
oysters ... fresh ... raw	2.4	80	300	134	0
smoked ... canned in oil	12	76	400	40	0
prawn chow mein	10.9	26	330	34	2
prawn cocktail	7.4	86	830	25	0.1
prawn cutlets	14.8	164	650	50	0
prawn omelette	15.6	173	480	45	tr
prawns ... cooked	0.9	188	480	135	0
garlic	7.4	190	490	100	0
rollmops	11.3	70	1270	100	0
salmon, pink/red ... canned ...					
in brine	10	65	530	200	0
no added salt	6.5	65	120	200	0
smoked	4.6	50	1710	15	0
sardines ... canned in brine	12	110	760	303	0
in oil	15.7	114	600	360	0
scallops ... simmered	1.4	61	150	27	0
shrimps ... fried in batter	10.8	190	186	72	0.4

*Values are given for 100g unless specified otherwise.	FAT g/ 100g⁺	CHOL mg/ 100g⁺	SOD mg/ 100g⁺	CALC mg/ 100g⁺	FIBRE* g/ 100g⁺

	FAT g/100g⁺	CHOL mg/100g⁺	SOD mg/100g⁺	CALC mg/100g⁺	FIBRE* g/100g⁺
spaghetti marinara	4.6	41	250	36	0.9
taramasalata	19.4	32	630	20	tr
tuna ... canned in brine	2.6	53	440	10	0
in oil	13.7	40	440	7	0
raw/canned ... no added salt	2	50	90	10	0
whiting ... floured ... pan-fried	6.2	98	70	30	tr
in batter ... deep-fried	19.6	114	460	40	0.6
steamed	1.1	94	70	30	0
Birds Eye ...					
light wholemeal crumbed fillets	10.5	20	181		
light 'n healthy lightly crumbed fillets	7.8		268		2.5
Findus Lean Cuisine ...					
fish in lemon sauce ... 1 sv ... 225g	13	100	1482		
Frelish ... patties	77		360	210	

Fruit and Fruit Foods

Fruit (fresh, canned, cooked, frozen or dried), without added ingredients, contains only a trace of fat, no cholesterol and very low levels of sodium and calcium. The fruits listed here are included for their significant contribution of dietary fibre to the diet.

*Values are given for 100g unless specified otherwise.	FAT g/ 100g+	CHOL mg/ 100g+	SOD mg/ 100g+	CALC mg/ 100g+	FIBRE* g/ 100g+
apple ... raw ... av type	tr	0	1	5	1.6
apricot ... raw/canned ... av type	tr	0	2	16	1.9
banana	tr	0	1	5	1.4
boysenberry ... John West ... canned	tr	0	3	5	3.3
cherry/grape	tr	0	5	10	0.7
date	tr	0	15	50	5.2
melon ... cantaloupe/honeydew	tr	0	25	25	0.6
nectarine	tr	0	1	10	1.5
orange	tr	0	2	30	1.4
passionfruit	tr	0	20	10	3.9
pawpaw	tr	0	7	30	1.1
peach ... canned	tr	0	5	5	1.9
peeled	tr	0	2	5	1.5
unpeeled	tr	0	2	5	2.1
pear ... canned	tr	0	3	5	2.8
peeled	tr	0	2	5	3.2
unpeeled	tr	0	2	5	.5
pineapple ... raw/canned ... av type	tr	0	3	10	1.2
plum	tr	0	2	10	1.2
prune	tr	0	10	50	4
strawberry	tr	0	5	15	0.9
watermelon	tr	0	2	10	0.3
jams ... av all varieties	0	0	15	15	1.3
orange juice	0	0	2	10	0.2
prune juice	0	0	3	142	0.8
raisins	tr	0	50	68	5
sultanas	tr	0	35	53	4

Meats

Animal foods (meat, fish, poultry, eggs, milk and dairy foods) by themselves contain no dietary fibre. Some sausages, hamburgers, luncheon meats and convenience meats are manufactured with added cereals and/or legumes, which may contribute small amounts of dietary fibre.

*Values are given for 100g unless specified otherwise.	FAT g/ 100g+	CHOL mg/ 100g+	SOD mg/ 100g+	CALC mg/ 100g+	FIBRE* g/ 100g+
bacon ... fried	30	74	1540	10	0
grilled	22	88	2000	10	0
beef ...					
cooked ... av trim	13.5	78	60	10	0
lean	6.3	75	60	9	0
chuck steak ... cooked ... av trim	13.7	86	45	7	0
lean	6	82	50	7	0
corned brisket ... boiled	24	70	820	6	0
corned silverside ... boiled ... av trim	12.9	70	1280	5	0
lean	3.5	70	1420	5	0
fillet steak ... grilled ... av trim	13.2	85	60	6	0
lean	8.3	82	60	6	0
hamburger mince ... cooked	12.1	93	62	15	0
kidney ... cooked	2.7	549	110	17	0
liver ... cooked	11.7	409	70	9	0
mince ... regular ... cooked	9.8	69	60	9	0

*Values are given for 100g unless specified otherwise.	FAT g/ 100g⁺	CHOL mg/ 100g⁺	SOD mg/ 100g⁺	CALC mg/ 100g⁺	FIBRE* g/ 100g⁺
oxtail	29.3	59	50	15	0
rump steak ... grilled ... av trim	16.8	86	50	5	0
lean	7	82	50	5	0
tongue ... simmered	25	60	80	6	0
topside roast ... baked ... av trim	10	68	50	5	0
lean	5	66	50	5	0
tripe ... stewed	4.5	160	73	150	0
beef in black-bean sauce	7.2	21	560	214	0.5
beef casserole with vegetables	11	30	330	14	2.4
beef chow mein	8.7	8	420	15	2.4
beef in oyster sauce	9.6	20	550	11	0.5
beef satay	12.9	23	450	18	2
beef sausage ... grilled	18	65	900	14	2.2
cannelloni	8.4	24	260	67	3
frozen	6.7	18	310	57	3
chicken ...					
breast ... with skin ... baked	12.7	99	60	10	0
without skin ... baked	4.8	92	65	10	0

+Values are given for 100g unless specified otherwise.	FAT g/ 100g+	CHOL mg/ 100g+	SOD mg/ 100g+	CALC mg/ 100g+	FIBRE* g/ 100g+
breast quarter roast ... with skin	12.3	75	180	10	0
cooked ... av trim ... with skin	16.3	128	75	14	0
without skin	8.1	128	80	16	0
croquette ... deep-fried ... 2	17.6	29	610	20	tr
drumstick ... with skin	15	151	91	20	0
without skin	10.6	154	96	20	0
leg quarter roast ... with skin	18.6	92	190	10	0
Kentucky/McDonald's see *Take-away and Convenience Meals*					
chicken a la king	14	80	310	52	1
chicken and almonds	9.8	46	430	28	1
chicken cacciatore	7.5	61	240	26	1
chicken chop suey	6.5	20	230	16	2.4
chicken, lemon ... crispy skin ... av sample	14	85	465	20	tr
chicken omelette	18	101	420	25	tr
corned beef see beef (above)					
dim sim	8.6	7	1070	67	1.3
duck, Chinese see *Take-away and Convenience Meals*					
duck, roast	29	150	200	20	0
frankfurters ... boiled	20	60	770	30	1.8
cocktail	24	60	360	6	1.5
ham ... canned ... leg	4.5	42	1250	14	0
shoulde	6.3	4	143	16	0
cooked ... leg	7.6	53	1515	8	0
shoulder	6	52	1270	9	0
hamburger ... plai	10.2	2	660	21	1.8
see also *Take-away and Convenience Meals*					
lamb ... brains ... simmered	9.4	1886	110	10	0
chump chops ... grilled ... av trim	18.4	109	70	20	0
lean	7.8	109	75	17	0
crumbed, fried	21.1	1900	380	43	0.4
cutlets ... crumbed, fried	38.2	109	500	9	0.4
kidney ... simmered	4.3	550	200	20	0

*Values are given for 100g unless specified otherwise.	FAT g/ 100g+	CHOL mg/ 100g+	SOD mg/ 100g+	CALC mg/ 100g+	FIBRE* g/ 100g+
leg ... baked ... av trim	11.9	109	70	5	0
lean	5.6	109	70	4	0
liver ... fried	13.7	585	100	7	0
midloin chops ... grilled ... av trim	31.4	110	90	8	0
75% trim	15.2	109	90	7	0
lean	7.2	109	100	7	0
shank	10.5	109	80	20	0
tongue ... simmered	20.4	146	90	9	0
lamb casserole with vegetables	7.9	100	350	12	2.4
lamb's fry and bacon ... fried	38.2	500	550	7	0
lasagne	6	18	240	39	2
Lebanese sausages	18.1	71	650	28	
luncheon meats ...					
beef, German	17.4	48	800	37	1
Berliner fleischwurst	18.2	60	750	26	1
black pudding	18.6	72	970	48	1
cabanossi	31.6	71	810	31	1
chicken Devon	17.8	64	920	38	1

*Values are given for 100g unless specified otherwise.	FAT g/ 100g+	CHOL mg/ 100g+	SOD mg/ 100g+	CALC mg/ 100g+	FIBRE* g/ 100g+
chicken roll	7.6	47	670	32	1.3
Devon	18	45	770	38	1
fritz	19	51	830	32	1
garlic roll	18.9	51	840	34	2.4
ham and chicken roll	18	50	800	30	1.7
ham sausage	23.8	67	630	21	1
liverwurst ... calf	26.2	140	700	23	1
chicken	26.4	130	670	21	1
mortadella	29.3	64	770	45	1.4
salami ... Danish	40.2	115	1370	23	0
Hungarian	37.4	92	1860	27	0
mettwurst	37.5	81	1470	18	0
Milano	36.9	104	1390	39	0
pepperoni	36.1	129	1200	25	0
Polish	17.8	50	880	19	0
Strasbourg	19.2	51	870	31	1.8
meat paste	13	90	800	200	1
meat pie see *Take-away and Convenience Meals*					
moussaka	9.6	40	310	70	0.9
osso bucco	9.6	77	310	37	0.5
pastie see *Take-away and Convenience Meals*					
pâté	24.7	159	970	24	1.3
pork ... butterfly steak ... grilled ... av trim	17.6	86	45	8	0
75% trim	8.4	84	50	8	0
lean	4.7	83	50	8	0
Chinese, barbecued	15.2	63	1070	18	tr
chop ... grilled	28	92	75	32	0
75% trim	14.4	92	80	30	0
chop suey	8.8	15	550	26	2.4
cooked ... av trim	22	89	60	14	0
leg ... baked ... av trim	26.7	15	50	6	0
75% trim	11.4	92	50	7	0

+Values are given for 100g unless specified otherwise.	FAT g/ 100g+	CHOL mg/ 100g+	SOD mg/ 100g+	CALC mg/ 100g+	FIBRE* g/ 100g+
sausage ... grilled	22	60	1000	15	1.5
spare ribs ... in black-bean sauce	14.6	38	800	36	0.5
in plum sauce	17.4	43	500	20	0.5
sweet-and-sour	9.4	60	390	14	1.5
steak ... grilled ... av trim	5.9	93	60	6	0
lean	5.2	84	60	13	0
ravioli	5.4	20	310	77	1.5
frozen	4.6	14	280	65	1.5
saltimbocca	14.1	59	500	77	0.4
sausage roll	17.6	20	650	20	1.3
sausages ... with meat ... deep-fried	25.2	48	800	13	0.4
grilled	17.3	60	810	14	2.8
saveloy ... in batter, deep-fried	20.8	23	1020	35	0.1
shish kebab	10	135	170	10	0
souvlakia	11.3	94	320	10	0
spaghetti Bolognese	4	10	240	29	1
turkey ... Tegel ... breast roll ... roasted	2.1	150	480	7	0
veal ... boneless ... cooked ... av trim	3.9	111	80	7	0
lean	2.5	111	80	7	0
chops ... grilled ... av trim	4.8	111	100	8	0
trimmed	2.3	82	90	8	0
cutlets ... crumbed, fried	28.5	110	211	4	0.4
kidney ... grilled	6.7	434	230	15	0

You don't have to buy full-cream milk to be sure that you get the valuable calcium it contains. Modified fat and skim milks are just as high in calcium as whole milk. They may have lost some of the A and D vitamins through having the fat skimmed off, but many producers are putting these lost vitamins back into their low-fat products. Even hardened whole-milk drinkers can make the transition to skim milk by changing to fat-modified milk first. If you use skim milk for cooking you will probably be unable to taste the difference.

*Values are given for 100g unless specified otherwise.	FAT g/ 100g+	CHOL mg/ 100g+	SOD mg/ 100g+	CALC mg/ 100g+	FIBRE* g/ 100g+
liver ... cooked	8.1	244	100	7	0
shank ... simmered	2.4	82	100	23	0
veal marsala	10.6	82	210	7	tr
Findus Lean Cuisine ... 1 sv ...					
beef oriental ... 245g	6	39	1270		
coconut chicken ... 260g	7	31	455		
spaghetti beef and mushroom ... 325g	5	20	530		

Milk, Ice-cream, Yoghurt and Non-dairy Substitutes

	FAT g/ 100g+	CHOL mg/ 100g+	SOD mg/ 100g+	CALC mg/ 100g+	FIBRE* g/ 100g+
coconut cream	20	0	20	4	1.7
coconut milk ... from fresh nut	tr	0	20	15	tr
cream/sour cream/thickened cream	35	100	36	60	0
cream ... reduced-fat	25	85	40	97	0
ice-cream ... vanilla ... tub variety	11	32	80	140	0
milk ... cow's, whole	3.8	14	51	120	0
flavoured ... av all varieties	3.5	14	55	110	0
goat's, UHT	2.6	9	66	110	0
human	3.9	16	14	31	0
low-cholesterol ... PhysiCAL Slim	0.1	5	38	215	0
low-fat ... Pauls Shape	0.15	3	69	163	0
reduced-fat ... PhysiCAL	1.4	5	38	205	0
REV	1.2	6	60	150	0
Big M ... av all flavours	3.1	11	55	116	0
Farm House	8	18	58	118	0
milk, condensed ... sweet. ... full-cream	9.2	27	104	250	0
skim	0.3	6	120	320	0
milk, evaporated ... unsweet. ... full-cream	8.1	20	100	250	0
skim	0.3	5	100	250	0
milk powder ... full-cream	26.2	6	300	780	0
skim	1	13	425	1310	0
rice drink ... Aussie Dream	1	0	62	1	2
sour cream ... reduced-fat	19.7	47	56	135	0

*Values are given for 100g unless specified otherwise.	FAT g/ 100g+	CHOL mg/ 100g+	SOD mg/ 100g+	CALC mg/ 100g+	FIBRE* g/ 100g+
sour-cream dip	17.4	36	600	130	0
soya curd/tofu ... fried	25	0	10	507	0.4
steamed	4	0	10	507	0.4
soya drink ... So Good ... plain	3.2	0	40	116	
yoghurt ... fruit ... av all flavours	2.1	8	65	130	0.2
low-fat	0.2	2	68	173	0.2
plain	4.4	14	77	195	0
low-fat	0.2	2	97	260	0
Everest ... choc tofu ice confection	3.2	6.9	43		
Streets ... cal control ...100-ml sv	1.2		48	62	0
cornetto ... wild strawb ... 1	11.9		66	1070	0
paddle pop ... van. ... 1	3.2		60	79.2	0
Vitari ... fruit ice ... av all flavours	tr	0	38	0	

Nuts and Seeds

	FAT g/ 100g+	CHOL mg/ 100g+	SOD mg/ 100g+	CALC mg/ 100g+	FIBRE* g/ 100g+
almonds ... roasted, salted	56.7	0	198	245	9
sugar-coated	18.6	0	20	100	8
brazil	68	0	2	180	9
cashew	45	0	11	50	5
coconut ... desiccated	62	0	13	23	15
fresh	36	0	20	13	7
peanut butter	50	0	300	45	10
Farmland ... no added salt	49	0	25	65	10
peanuts ... raw	47.9	0	4	57	9
roasted, salted	48.6	0	440	72	8
Farmland ... no added salt	51	0	10	65	1.9
sesame seeds	55	0	24	60	10
sunflower seeds	51	0	tr	100	10
tahini paste	60	0	80	330	13

see also **Snack Foods**

+Values are given for 100g unless specified otherwise.	FAT g/ 100g+	CHOL mg/ 100g+	SOD mg/ 100g+	CALC mg/ 100g+	FIBRE* g/ 100g+

Salad Dressings

	FAT	CHOL	SOD	CALC	FIBRE
French dressing ... av brand	35.2	0	1200	7	0.5
Italian dressing ... Bertolli/Kraft	26.7	0	865	12	1.2
mayonnaise ... home-made ... av sample	78.9	90	360	20	0.5
low-energy, low-oil ... av all brands	0.9	0	890	36	1
Fountain Salad Magic ... cholesterol-free	10	0	1200		0
Gold'n Canola	15	1	780		0
Hain	81.7	14	360	20	0.6
Kraft ... coleslaw	35	44	1855		0.5
French	0	0	1610		
Italian	30	0	1652		
miracle whip	51.1	81	190		0.7
natural	27.5	32	800		0.5
Praise ... light	15	1	780		0
no-cholesterol	35	0	776		0

*Values are given for 100g unless specified otherwise.	FAT g/ 100g+	CHOL mg/ 100g+	SOD mg/ 100g+	CALC mg/ 100g+	FIBRE* g/ 100g+
salad dressing ...					
condensed-milk, home-made	5	14	840	90	0
thousand island ... av sample	36	28	840	10	1.4

Salt, Sauces, Gravies and Seasonings

Most of the foods and condiments in this section are included for the comparison of their sodium values. Unless indicated otherwise, they contain no significant levels of the other nutrients listed in these tables.

	FAT	CHOL	SOD	CALC	FIBRE
baking powder	0	0	11600	11300	0
1 tsp	0	0	580	565	0
beef extract	0.2	tr	6400	100	0
bicarbonate of soda	0	0	26000		0
1 tsp	0	0	1300		0
chutney ... av sample	0.5	0	650	25	2
1 tsp	tr	0	40	1	tr
curry powder	tr	0	450	640	
1 tsp	tr	0	22	32	
gravy ... made from roast-meat drippings	8.5	23	470	3	
gravy powder ... made up ... 1/4 cup	0.1	0	630	3	
1 tsp ... dry ... av sample	0.4	0	250	tr	0
marmite	1.6	0	3050	25	0
1 tsp	tr	0	152	.5	0
meat/chicken seasoning	tr	0	17600	70	0
meat tenderiser	tr	0	28000		0
1 tsp	tr	0	1400		0
monosodium glutamate (msg)	0	0	12500		0
1 tsp	0	0	700		0
mustard ... hot ... English	3	0	4400	80	4
prepared ... av sample	3	0	1500	80	4
mustard powder ... 1 tsp ... dry ... av sample	.2	0	240	20	tr
pepper/herbs/spices ... in normal use			tr		

*Values are given for 100g unless specified otherwise.	FAT g/100g+	CHOL mg/100g+	SOD mg/100g+	CALC mg/100g+	FIBRE* g/100g+
salt ... cooking/sea/table	0	0	39000	30	0
rock	0	0	39000	230	0
vegetable/celery/garlic	0	0	28000	20	0
1 tsp	0	0	2000	tr	0
salt-free substitutes	0	0	tr		0
salt substitute ... lite salt	0	0	20000		0
1 tsp	0	0	1000		0
*sauces** ... barbecue	tr	0	815	15	1
cheese	13	30	546	280	0.5
chilli	0.6	0	1338	9	1
curry, home-made	2.1	5	376	11	1
parsley, home-made	8	21	300	160	0.5
satay	10.6	0	500	40	2.5
soya	1.3	0	7500	20	0
low-salt	1	0	3400	20	0
tartare	53.8	90	707	19	1
tomato	0.4	0	1042	20	1.9
Farmland ... no added salt	0.4	0	35	20	1.5
White Crow... no added salt			12		
white	8.9	21	300	160	tr
worcestershire ... Holbrooks	tr	0	690	160	0
sauces, dehydrated ... Bolognese	11.4		11300	45	tr
brown onion	10.7		13500	140	3
curry	13.2		10600	200	1
mushroom	11.2		12500	140	4
white	13		10800	600	tr
stock cubes and powders ... av	9	tr	10000	70	0
stuffing, savoury ... for chicken	8.4	13	520	30	2
tomato paste	tr	0	400	30	3

*For 1 tbsp of these sauces calculate one-fifth of values given – a useful approximate measurement.

*Values are given for 100g unless specified otherwise.	FAT g/ 100g+	CHOL mg/ 100g+	SOD mg/ 100g+	CALC mg/ 100g+	FIBRE* g/ 100g+
vegemite	tr	0	3200	50	0
1 tsp	tr	0	150	2	0
vinegar	0	0	tr	tr	0

Snack Foods

	FAT	CHOL	SOD	CALC	FIBRE
beer nuts					
salted	50	0	330		2
Farmland … no added salt	51	0	10	50	2.1
Nobby's salted peanuts	51.9	tr	540	40	5.8
corn chips … flavoured	29	2	640	120	5
toasted	26.7	0	600	110	4.9
extruded snack foods … cheese	27.9	8	1002	120	2.7
French fries	31.3	0	660	25	4.5
pappadums … CCA	27.4	tr	1670		8.9
popcorn … plain	24.4	6	980	9	8.5
pork rind snack	28.5	75	4260	17	0
potato crisps … cheese and onion	35	3	470	60	3.5
flavoured	33.4	1	460	37	3.5
plain	32.1	0	638	25	3.6
Farmland … no added salt	37	0	20	30	0.2
Lites … plain	33.5	0	590	30	5.6
chicken	28.9	1	310	30	3.5
potato straws … plain	31.3	0	660	31	3
pretzels … av sample	7.2	0	1980	25	3
CC's tangy bbq flavoured corn chips	23.7	tr	740	115	6.8

Soups

	FAT	CHOL	SOD	CALC	FIBRE
canned, condensed … av all varieties	3	tr	810	20	tr
chicken noodle … made up	tr	2	1136	5	tr
cream of chicken … canned, condensed	2.7	tr	710	20	tr
diluted with water	1.3	tr	350	10	tr
dried, packet mix … av all varieties	3	9	6120	40	tr

*Values are given for 100g unless specified otherwise.	FAT g/ 100g+	CHOL mg/ 100g+	SOD mg/ 100g+	CALC mg/ 100g+	FIBRE* g/ 100g+
tomato ... canned, condensed	tr	0	810	10	2
diluted with water	tr	0	410	5	1
Rosella ... diluted with half milk half water ...					
beef goulash	1.2		460		
chicken and corn	1.7		255		
pea and ham ... salt-reduced	1.3		103		

Take-away and Convenience Meals

	FAT g/ 100g+	CHOL mg/ 100g+	SOD mg/ 100g+	CALC mg/ 100g+	FIBRE* g/ 100g+
bean salad	4.8	0	450	20	3.7
cannelloni	6.7	21	285	60	3.3
chiko roll	10.4	7	690	30	1.3
Chinese duck	7.4	40	400	25	tr
Chinese fried rice	6.3	30	500	10	2
coleslaw see Kentucky (below)					
combination chow mein	9.5	40	410	12	2

+Values are given for 100g unless specified otherwise.	FAT g/ 100g+	CHOL mg/ 100g+	SOD mg/ 100g+	CALC mg/ 100g+	FIBRE* g/ 100g+
croissant with egg, cheese and bacon	22	167	689	117	1.5
dim sim ... fried	8.6	7	1070	60	1.3
fish cake see **Fish and Fish Foods**					
fish in batter see **Fish and Fish Foods**					
hamburger ... bacon	13.1	29	780	20	1.7
cheese	13.3	34	760	83	1.7
egg	11.8	110	600	26	1.6
plain	10.2	26	660	21	1.8
see also **Meats**; **McDonald's** (below)					
hot dog ... 1 av	24		900	30	1.2
lasagne see **Meats**					
meat pie	13.8	20	600	11	1.1
1 ... 170g	23	34	1000	18	1.8
Mexican ... enchirito + cheese, beef and beans	8.3	26	648	113	1
frijoles with cheese	4.7	22	528	113	2.3
nachos with cheese	16.8	16	722	241	1.7
taco	12	33	469	129	1.2
with chilli con carne	5	2	339	94	2
with salad	7.5	22	385	97	1.3
pastie	6.8	17	640	18	1.3
1 ... 165g	1.1	28	1000	30	2
pizza ... ham and pineapple ... frozen ... av sample	11.1	14	700	140	2.6
pizza supreme ... frozen ... av sample	11.5	20	720	160	2.6
potato, baked ... + cheese and bacon	8.7	10	325	103	0.5
+ sour cream and					

It has been a popular misconception that bread and potatoes are the most fattening foods. To gain 1 kg of body fat a person would need to eat more than 120 smallish (100-g) potatoes. The potato becomes the dieter's enemy only if accompanied by butter, margarine, sour cream, oil or some other type of fat.

*Values are given for 100g unless specified otherwise.	FAT g/100g⁺	CHOL mg/100g⁺	SOD mg/100g⁺	CALC mg/100g⁺	FIBRE* g/100g⁺
chives	7.4	8	60	35	0.5
potato chips	14	12	250	10	3.7
potato salad see Kentucky (below)					
potato scallop ... deep-fried	21.6	21	260	17	3
ravioli see Meats					
sausage roll	17.6	20	650	20	1.3
spaghetti in meat sauce ... canned	2.3	4	510	8	0.9
spaghetti in tomato/cheese sauce ...					
canned	0.4	1	400	9	0.9
spanakopita (spinach and cheese pie)	20.6	32	750	90	1.3
spring roll ... fried	9.8	11	780	26	1.3
steak sandwich	6.9	36	391	30	1.3
tofu burger	8		130		
Farmland ... *Irish stew* ... no added salt	2.4	30	110	12	1.5
Kentucky ... bacon and cheese chicken					
fillet burger	13.4				0.5
bean salad	4.8	0	450	19	
chicken fillet burger	13.3				0.6
chicken original recipe	22	98	440	15	
coleslaw	4	12	270	35	
Colonel Burger	12.9				0.5
French fries	16.3	5	60		
small sv	19.7	6	73		
Kentucky nuggets	16.4				
mashed potato and gravy ... 1	4.6	12	386	7	
potato salad	5.7	9	380	10	
medium sv	22.5	35	1500	38	
works burger	11.1				0.7
McDonald's ... apple pie ... 1	17.5	17	197	19	
big breakfast ... 1	33.9	433	840	140	1.1
big mac ... 1	26.9	66.7	1092	153	1.1
cheeseburger ... 1	16	35	815	104	1.3

*Values are given for 100g unless specified otherwise.	FAT g/100g[+]	CHOL mg/100g[+]	SOD mg/100g[+]	CALC mg/100g[+]	FIBRE* g/100g[+]
chicken mcnuggets ...					
6 pieces with sauce	20.7	114	630	31	
cookies ... 1 box	12.5	10	132	22	1.5
English muffin ... 1	6.4	12.2	200	61	2.4
filet-o-fish ... 1	16.7	38	962	80	1.4
French fries ...					
regular ... 81g	12.6	17	123	7	2.4
hashbrown ... 1	12.6	22	290		
hotcakes with syrup ... 1	11.8	30	1130	120	
junior burger	11.4	22	193	12	0.1
mcfeast	30.9	76	896	65	0.8
milk shake ... van. regular	10.9	88	210	210	0
quarter pounder + cheese	35.7	76	1380	12	0.8
sausage mcmuffin ... 1	18.7	53	540	170	
scrambled egg and muffin	20.6	382	610	100	1.1
sundae ... 1	7	11	120	160	0
Pizza Hut ... pan ... supreme ...					
1 slice ... 136g	16.2		775		2.7
thin'n crispy ... cheese ...					
1 slice ... 79g	9.1		498		1.6

Ratatouille

225 g eggplant, sliced
1 tablespoon oil
1 medium-sized onion, sliced
1 level teaspoon crushed garlic
300 g zucchini, sliced

1 green capsicum, seeded and sliced
225 g tomatoes, sliced
2 level tablespoons dried thyme
salt and pepper to taste
1 level teaspoon finely chopped parsley

Cook eggplant in boiling water for 10 minutes and then drain. Heat oil in a non-stick pan and fry onion and garlic until soft. Add eggplant and fry for another 2 minutes. Add zucchini, capsicum, tomato and thyme to onion and eggplant mixture. Season to taste. Cover and simmer for 20 minutes. Stir in parsley and cook for a further 5 minutes. Makes 2 servings at 695 kJ (165 Cal) per portion.

+Values are given for 100g unless specified otherwise.	FAT g/ 100g+	CHOL mg/ 100g+	SOD mg/ 100g+	CALC mg/ 100g+	FIBRE* g/ 100g+

Vegetables and Vegetable Foods

	FAT	CHOL	SOD	CALC	FIBRE
artichoke, Jerusalem ... boiled	tr	0	5	20	3.2
asparagus ... boiled	tr	0	2	20	2.1
canned	tr	0	295	10	1
Farmland ... no added salt	tr	0	5	10	0.8
aubergine (eggplant) ... baked	tr	0	5	20	3.5
avocado	22.6	0	2	20	1.5
baked beans ... Heinz ... canned	0.7	0	385	30	5
salt-reduced	0.7	0	270	30	5
beans ... 4-bean mix ... canned	tr	0	150	20	4
green ... canned	tr	0	330	30	2
raw/boiled/frozen	tr	0	2	30	2.2
red kidney ... boiled	tr	0	8	34	7
canned	tr	0	320	36	6.5
beetroot ... canned	tr	0	236	8	2.8
broccoli ... boiled	tr	0	20	31	3.7
brussels sprouts ... boiled	tr	0	30	14	2.9
cabbage ... boiled	tr	0	20	24	1.6
capsicum, green ... raw	tr	0	2	8	1.3
carrot ... raw ... av type	tr	0	40	30	3
carrots ... canned	tr	0	148	30	2.5
no added salt	tr	0	50	30	2.5
cauliflower ... av	tr	0	14	13	2.1
celery ... raw	tr	0	90	36	1.3
corn see *sweetcorn* (below)					
cucumber ... peeled		0	20	13	0.4
pickled	tr	0	1353	20	2.2
unpeeled	tr	0	20	13	1.1
felafel	14.9	0	610	68	3.5

*Values are given for 100g unless specified otherwise.	FAT g/100g+	CHOL mg/100g+	SOD mg/100g+	CALC mg/100g+	FIBRE* g/100g+
gherkin ... pickled	tr	0	1000	20	2.2
homous	17.1	0	310	45	3
leek ... boiled	tr	0	20	30	2.9
lentils ... boiled	tr	0	10	20	3.7
lettuce	tr	0	23	16	1.7
mushrooms ... raw	tr	0	7	2	2.5
olives ... black ... pickled	21.2	0	900	100	1
green ... pickled	12.9	0	2480	76	8
onion ... fried	20	0	15	24	1.5
raw	tr	0	13	18	1.5
spring	tr	0	13	22	2.2
parsley	tr	0	50	200	4.7
parsnip ... boiled	tr	0	20	36	2.5
peas ... canned	tr	0	230	27	7.4
Farmland ... no added salt	tr	0	5	27	7
fresh ... boiled	tr	0	1	18	6.5
frozen ... boiled ... av type	tr	0	3	27	5.8
potato ... chips ... fried	14.2	12	160	10	1.2
frozen, fried	12.2	10	300	10	1.2
dehydrated ... made up	2.3	1	240	40	3.6
mashed with full-cream milk	0.4	3	300	10	1.2
salad	9.2	7	380	10	1.2
scallop ... deep-fried	21.6	21	260	17	3
pumpkin ... boiled ... av type	tr	0	1	20	2.1
silver beet ... boiled ... no added salt	tr	0	185	68	2.5
spinach ... boiled	tr	0	20	50	1.9
swede ... boiled	tr	0	12	20	3.4

Raw onions have an energy value of 30 kJ (7 Cal) per 30 g; sliced and fried they soar to 190 kJ (45 Cal). If a recipe requires that chopped onions be pre-fried, poach them instead in a little liquid until softened.

*Values are given for 100g unless specified otherwise.	FAT g/ 100g+	CHOL mg/ 100g+	SOD mg/ 100g+	CALC mg/ 100g+	FIBRE* g/ 100g+
sweetcorn ... boiled on the cob	1.9	0	5	3	1.7
canned	0.6	0	260	4	2.7
Farmland ... no added salt	1	0	5	3	2.7
frozen ... cooked	1	0	5	3	2.6
kernels ... cooked	1.2	0	5	3	4.8
sweet potato	tr	0	10	26	1.8
tomato ... canned	tr	0	230	98	0.8
no added salt	tr	0	5–20	9	0.8
raw	tr	0	6	8	1.3
tomato juice ... canned	tr	0	230	7	1
low-salt	tr	0	1–20	7	1
tomato paste	1	0	160	15	3
Farmland ... no added salt	1	0	60	15	3.3
tomato puree	tr	0	350	12	2
turnip ... boiled	tr	0	20	20	2.5
vine leaves	2.9	0	600	60	2.5
Birds Eye ... vegetable bakes	7.5	0.3	395		5.3
vegetable fingers	2.3		126		1.7

VITAMIN GUIDE

VITAMINS AND WHY WE NEED THEM

The food we eat, besides supplying us with our food energy, supplies many other essential nutrients on a much smaller scale. Vitamins are among them.

- Vitamins are chemical compounds needed in small amounts to promote growth, vitality and general well-being. Most vitamins cannot be made in the body, but must be supplied in our diet.

- The best way for a healthy person to obtain vitamins is to eat a daily diet that includes a variety of foods from each of the basic food groups (see p.10). Including foods such as green, leafy and yellow vegetables, legumes, fruits, nuts, cereals, seafood, poultry, lean meat and dairy products will ensure an adequate intake of all vitamins and minerals.

- A Recommended Dietary Intake (**RDI**) has been established for most vitamins. In order to provide a margin of safety, the RDI is considerably greater than the amount actually needed daily for good health (see tables for individual vitamins, pp. 221–233).

WHEN CAN VITAMIN DEFICIENCIES OCCUR?

During various stages in life and because of various illnesses, your vitamin needs may change. Examples are:

- during chronic stress and illness
- when recovering from illness or surgery
- if you are on certain long-term medications (for example antibiotics, laxatives, L-dopa, hydralzine, isoniazid, Warfarin)
- if you are taking an oral contraceptive
- during pregnancy and breastfeeding
- if during your menstruation years you cut down or eliminate meat from your diet without increasing other food sources of iron
- if you are over 60 years of age, living and eating alone and with a poor appetite
- if you are a teenager or young adult with a desire to be slim and have reduced your calorie intake to below 3350–4200 kilojoules (800–1000 calories) a day
- if you are a vegetarian who does not consume dairy products or eggs and particularly if pregnant or breastfeeding
- if you skip meals and snack on high-sugar and high-fat foods
- if you regularly go on fad diets that leave out complete food groups
- if you are drinking heavily (more than 40 grams of alcohol per day) on a regular basis
- if you smoke heavily.

SUPPLEMENTS – NOT SUBSTITUTES

In Australia where the food supply is abundant, vitamin-deficiency diseases are seldom seen. Despite this, about one in four Australians regularly take vitamin supplements – usually 'just to be sure'. Some people think that as long as they take vitamin supplements they don't have to worry about what they eat. You need to be aware of the following.

- Vitamins are neither pep pills nor substitutes for food. Food contains a variety of nutrients; vitamins are just one part of them. You cannot take vitamin supplements, stop eating and expect to be healthy.

- Some vitamins are toxic in large amounts. Self-treatment of real or suspected diseases with large doses of vitamins may be dangerous. It can also lead to a false sense of security and delay appropriate medical attention.

Research shows that the average Australian is confused about vitamins. The idea that vitamins have almost miraculous powers still persists. The following section on specific vitamins will shed some light on what they can and cannot do for you.

VITAMINS AND FREE RADICALS

Free radicals are potentially toxic particles produced in the body in very small amounts. Three vitamins, beta-carotene (one of the forms of vitamin A), vitamin C and vitamin E, are able to neutralise or deactivate these toxins under certain circumstances.

VITAMIN A

Vitamin A is present in food in two main forms:

- as retinol (the vitamin itself), found mostly in foods of animal origin, such as dairy products, egg yolk and liver
- as beta-carotene, which is converted to retinol in our intestines. Most of our vitamin A is supplied in the beta-carotene form, mainly in yellow, orange and dark-green plant foods.

Our bodies are good at storing vitamin A; most people have enough in store for 1–2 years. Therefore it is not crucial to replenish it every day.

FOOD SOURCES	Retinol mcg*/100g	Beta-carotene mcg*/100g
Liver (fried)	35,400	60
Cod liver oil	1800	1050
Cheese (cheddar)	350	210
Egg yolk	430	0
Carrot (raw)	0	10,350
Spinach (frozen, boiled)	0	6810
Sweet potato	0	5760
Pumpkin	0	2680

Notes
- Large doses of retinol can be toxic, especially during pregnancy, so don't take chances with massive doses in supplement form. You can get all you need by eating a variety of foods, including yellow, orange or dark-green vegetables most days.

Function
- Essential part of visual purple in the eye that is responsible for seeing in dim light.
- Maintains healthy skin and lining in the lung and intestines, is essential for normal bone formation, supports resistance to infection and has antioxidant properties.

Deficiency
- Night blindness, dry eyes and skin, increased susceptibility to infection.

Who is at risk?
- Alcoholics, and people with malabsorption disorders or severe liver disease.

Toxicity
- One massive dose or large doses over a long period can cause appetite and hair loss, headaches, blurred vision, dry and flaky skin, liver damage, and death in extreme cases.
- Carotenes are not toxic, but continued doses 5–10 times the RDI are not advisable.

RDI: 750 mcg of retinol or 4500 mcg beta-carotene daily.

mcg = micrograms

VITAMIN D

Vitamin D is typically found in dairy products, but the body can make its own by the action of sunlight on skin. In Australia where there is adequate sunlight a deficiency is very rare: just a few minutes in the sunshine every other day will provide this vitamin. Vitamin D is involved in making bones and is very important for body calcium.

FOOD SOURCES	Vitamin D mcg*/100g
Liver (fried)	210
Fatty fish	5–25
Margarine	8
Egg yolk	5
Butter	1
Cheese	0.2
Milk	0.01

Notes
- Symptoms of toxic overdose are rare but very serious: parts of the body calcify.
- The margin between enough and too much is believed to be less than for any other vitamin.

Function
- Necessary for the body to absorb and use calcium, a major component of bones and teeth.

Deficiency
- Poor bone and tooth development in children (rickets).
- Loss of calcium from bones in adults (osteomalacia).

Who is at risk?
- Infants, young children, the elderly or invalids, if not exposed to sunlight.
- People with malabsorption syndromes and liver and kidney diseases.

Toxicity
- Loss of appetite, headache, nausea, vomiting, intense thirst.
- Irreversible damage to lung and kidneys may result.

RDI: No recommendation is made since Australians obtain sufficient amounts from sunlight on skin, without needing any from food.

* mcg = micrograms

VITAMIN E

Vitamin E originates from plants and has important antioxidant functions. While wheatgerm oil and vegetable oils are the best sources of this vitamin, it is found in almost every type of food. It is very difficult and unpalatable to eat a diet deficient in vitamin E and perhaps this is why deficiences are very rare.

Many claims are made about this vitamin, including an ability to increase physical endurance, exhance sexual potency, prevent heart attacks and slow the ageing process. Most of these claims are not proven.

FOOD SOURCES	Vitamin E mg/100g
Wheatgerm oil	130
Sunflower oil	49
Safflower oil	39
Margarine	25
Almonds	20
Wheatgerm	11
Tuna (canned)	6
Olive oil	5

Notes
- Polyunsaturated fats increase our need for vitamin E to prevent fat oxidation. But since most of these fats also contain vitamin E, extra is automatically supplied with their use.

Function
- Antioxidant: protects polyunsaturated fats and other oxygen-sensitive compounds, such as vitamins A and C, from undesirable oxidation and damage from free radicals.
- Works with selenium to protect against damage to cells by various substances that come from body chemistry, and from environmental pollutants, which tend to damage body cells.
- Has a role in the healing of wounds.

Deficiency
- Deficiency is unknown in people who eat a usual mixed diet.

Who is at risk?
- Infants with low birth weight.
- People with malabsorption syndromes.

Toxicity
- Large doses can be used by most people without harmful effects.
- Reports of muscle weakness and flu-like symptoms in some people taking large doses over long periods of time.

RDI: 7–10 mg (15 International Units) of vitamin E (as alpha tocopheral) daily.

VITAMIN K

Vitamin K is found in green plants and is also made by the bacteria inside our intestines. Deficiency of this vitamin in adults is rare, probably because the intestinal bacteria constantly produce a supply and the amount the body needs is very small. A varied diet provides approximately 300–500 mcg of vitamin K daily. This is more than adequate.

FOOD SOURCES	Vitamin K mcg*/100g
Spinach	240
Broccoli	200
Cabbage	125
Wheat bran	80
Green beans	20
Pork liver	25

Notes
- Taking antibiotics over a long period of time can kill off the bacteria that normally live in our intestines, resulting in a reduction in vitamin K production. A normal diet with a slightly increased amount of green vegetables will easily make up the deficit.

Function
- Ensures normal clotting of blood.

Deficiency
- Haemorrhaging may occur because the time that blood takes to clot is delayed.

Who is at risk?
- Newborn infants.
- People with malabsorption syndromes and liver diseases.
- Certain antibiotics and anticoagulant therapy may increase risk of deficiency.

Toxicity
- Excessive amounts can cause red blood cells to rupture and release substances that accumulate in the blood and brain, causing serious damage.

RDI: No recommendations have been made in Australia but estimated daily requirement is about 2mcg/kg body mass.

* mcg = micrograms

THIAMIN

Thiamin (vitamin B_1) is widely distributed in foods but in relatively small amounts in most of them. Thiamin is directly related to the amount of food energy we take in: the more kilojoules or calories eaten, the more thiamin needed. High-carbohydrate diets also increase our requirement for thiamin, but it is readily provided when the carbohydrate comes from complex carbohydrates such as wholegrain breads and cereals, and starchy vegetables. Because the refining of cereal products removes much of the thiamin, bread and cereal products have thiamin added to ensure that daily requirements are met.

FOOD SOURCES	Thiamin mg/100g
Brewers yeast	13
Yeast extract	11
Meat extract	9.1
Wheatgerm	1.5
Sesame seeds	1
Unprocessed bran	0.9
Enriched breakfast cereals	0.9
Green peas	0.3
Almonds	0.2

Notes
- If your diet contains more than the average amounts of alcohol, sugar and fats, you may need more thiamin. Eat more wholegrain breads and cereals, nuts, lean pork, vegemite and fresh green leafy vegetables.

Function
- Involved in many chemical reactions in the body, which release energy, and from carbohydrate in particular, but also from protein and fat. But thiamin itself cannot supply energy or cure 'that tired, run-down feeling', as is often claimed.

Deficiency
- Serious deficiency is known as beri-beri, with loss of appetite and muscle tone, vomiting, fatigue, nerve degeneration, mental confusion and heart failure.

Who is at risk?
- Alcoholics.
- People who regularly consume large amounts of alcohol.

Toxicity
- Large doses in tablet form appear to be safe but when taken intravenously have produced symptoms of toxic shock.

RDI: 1.1 mg of thiamin or 0.1 mg per 1000 kJ/240 Cal daily.

RIBOFLAVIN

Riboflavin (vitamin B_2) is found in a wide variety of animal and vegetable sources in small amounts. Sources include milk, dairy products, breakfast cereals, liver, kidney, yeast, green vegetables, fish and eggs. Riboflavin is a very sensitive to sunlight. Milk may lose at least half its riboflavin content if exposed to light for about two hours.

FOOD SOURCES	Riboflavin mg/100g
Yeast extract	16
Lamb's liver	4.4
Kidney	2.3
Chicken liver	1.7
Milk powder	1.5
Enriched breakfast cereals	1.3
Cheese (camembert)	0.6
Milk (whole)	0.5

Notes
- If you eat little meat or milk and dairy products you should increase your intake of these foods or have more of the other sources of riboflavin, e.g. soy drinks and breakfast cereals (including muesli).

Function
- Functions as part of a group of enzymes involved in release of energy from protein, carbohydrates and fat.

Deficiency
- Cracking of lips and at angles of mouth, swelling of the tongue.
- In children, failure to grow.
- Visual disturbance.

Who is at risk?
- Deficiency is rare in Australia and is associated with deficiency of other B-group vitamins.

Toxicity
- No toxic or adverse reactions have been reported.

RDI: 1.2 – 1.7 mg of riboflavin daily, depending on food-energy requirements.

NIACIN

Niacin (vitamin B_3) is a member of the B-complex family of vitamins. Using the amino acid tryptophan, the body can make its own niacin – but not if the body doesn't have enough vitamin B_1, B_2, and B_6. Good sources of niacin are listed in the table below.

FOOD SOURCES	Niacin mg/100g
Yeast extract	110
Bran breakfast cereals	49
Peanuts	16
Tuna (canned)	12
Lamb's liver	9.6
Enriched breakfast cereals	9.2
Chicken	8
Veal	7
Steak	6.4

Notes
- High doses can precipitate diabetes and gout: treat vitamin supplements with caution.

Function
- Aids in the metabolism of proteins, carbohydrates and fats.
- Doses of 100–200 times the RDI are sometimes used as medication, under medical supervision only, for lowering blood cholesterol and triglycerides, and increasing high-density lipoprotein, which appears to be protective against heart disease.

Deficiency
Serious deficiency is characterised by the three Ds:
- dementia
- diarrhoea
- dermatitis.

Who is at risk?
- Deficiency is not a problem in Australia, though pregnant and lactating women need slightly more than usual.

Toxicity
- Essentially non-toxic, except for side effects resulting from doses above 1–4 g, such as flushing, arrhythmia and liver toxicity.

RDI: 10–20 mg of niacin daily.

PANTOTHENIC ACID

Pantothenic acid (vitamin B_5) is so common in our food supply that symptoms of deficiency are not ordinarily seen. Personality changes, irritability, restlessness, fatigue and muscle cramps have been observed under experimental conditions or after periods of extreme food restriction.

FOOD SOURCES	Pantothenic acid mg/100g
Yeast extract	8.9
Lamb's liver	7.6
Chicken liver	5.5
Broad beans	3.8
Skim-milk powder	3.5
Peanuts	2.7
Unprocessed bran	2.4
Bran breakfast cereals	1.7
Eggs	1.6
Watermelon	1.6
Cheese	1.4

Notes
- The usual mixed diet provides 5–20 mg, which is more than enough to meet the body's needs.

Function
Involved in:
- energy release from the metabolism of carbohydrates, proteins and fats
- formation of red blood cells
- formation of neurotransmitters.

Deficiency
Under experimental conditions only, the following may occur:
- personality changes
- irritability, restlessness
- fatigue, vomiting and muscle cramps.

Who is at risk?
- Dietary deficiency of this vitamin has not been recognised in humans.

Toxicity
- Toxicity is low but daily doses above 20 mg in the form of supplements may result in diarrhoea and fluid retention in susceptible individuals.

RDI: Not established, but 4–7 mg of pantothenic acid daily is considered safe and adequate.

PYRIDOXINE

Pyridoxine (vitamin B_6) is widely distributed in a variety of animal and plant food sources.

Your requirement of pyridoxine depends in part on the amount of protein in your diet. Generally, a single serve of chicken, meat or fish will supply the amount needed daily. True deficiency in Australia is very rare because the vitamin is so widely distributed in foods.

Pyridoxine deficiency is nevertheless easy to sell because symptoms are ill defined and similar to common health problems.

FOOD SOURCES	Pyridoxine mg/100g
Unprocessed bran	1.4
Breakfast cereals	0.8
Walnuts	0.6
Bananas	0.5
Liver	0.5
Tuna (canned)	0.4
Avocado	0.4
Lean meats	0.3

Notes
- You can become dependent on pyridoxine, particularly if you take supplements of 200–300 mg daily for over a month, and unpleasant reactions can occur when you stop the dosage.

Function
- Involved in the manufacture of proteins and release of energy from carbohydrates and fat.

Deficiency
- True deficiency is rare.
- Symptoms are vague but include: irritability, sleeplessness, depression, dermatitis and other skin problems, and susceptibility to infection.

Who is at risk?
- Alcohol abusers.
- Those who suddenly stop taking very large doses of the vitamin.
- Women on oral contraceptives (particularly high-oestrogen contraceptives).

Toxicity
- Toxicity is low.
- Symptoms of toxic overdose include unstable gait, numb feet, loss of hand control.
- Large doses can interfere with L-dopa, which is used to treat Parkinson's disease.

RDI: 0.8 – 1.9 mg of pyridoxine daily.

BIOTIN

Biotin (once called vitamin H) is important for many metabolic processes in the body. It is present in a wide variety of food sources. Significant amounts of biotin are produced by gut bacteria, which makes the dietary requirement uncertain.

FOOD SOURCES	Biotin mg/100g
Bakers yeast	200
Chicken liver	170
Soya beans	60
Eggs	25
Rolled oats	20
Oysters	10
Wholemeal bread	6
Salmon (canned)	5
Tuna (canned)	3

Notes
- An average, varied diet is likely to contain 50–300 mg per day. This meets the needs of most healthy adults.

Function
- Essential for manufacture of fatty acids.
- Involved in metabolism of amino acids and carbohydrates.
- Helps maintain healthy skin and hair.

Deficiency
- Extremely rare, but symptoms include lethargy, loss of appetite, nausea, vomiting, depression, dry skin and muscle pain.

Who is at risk?
- Biotin deficiency does not occur in humans unless brought on by eating excessive numbers of raw eggs.

Toxicity
- Toxicity is low.

RDI: Not developed, but 100–200 mg of biotin daily is considered safe and adequate.

COBALAMIN

Cobalamin (vitamin B_{12}) is present in all animal foods. Most plants contain no vitamin B_{12}. Strict vegetarians get small amounts from the microbes that grow naturally on some plant foods. This vitamin needs a substance produced by the stomach (a hormone called **intrinsic factor**) for its absorption, and the lack of it is the usual cause of deficiency. The body is good at storing vitamin B_{12} and is also efficient at recycling it; so only small amounts are required. Deficiency symptoms take up to 10 years to develop and are rarely seen within two years.

FOOD SOURCES	Cobalamin mcg*/100g
Lamb's liver (fried)	81
Sardines	28
Oysters	15
Egg yolk	5
Tuna (canned)	5
Turkey	3
Beef	1–2
Cheese (cheddar)	1.5

Notes
- The RDI for vitamin B_{12} is small and easily met by most diets. However, strict vegetarians should probably take a vitamin B_{12} supplement once or twice a week, particularly if pregnant or breastfeeding.

Function
- Involved in the manufacture of the gene-containing material of cells (DNA and RNA) and the substance that covers nerve cells (myelin).

Deficiency
- Pernicious anaemia results from inability to absorb vitamin B_{12}.
- Dietary deficiency is rare.

Who is at risk?
- Strict vegetarians.
- Newborn infants of vegetarian mothers.
- People who have had surgical removal of stomach.

Toxicity
- Very low toxicity.
- Oral supplements are considered safe and effective only for preventing dietary deficiency in strict vegetarians.

RDI: 2 mcg daily. An additional 1 – 1.5 mcg is required during pregnancy and breastfeeding.

mcg = micrograms

FOLATE

Folate is a B-group vitamin necessary for the production of blood cells and genetic material. Overall folate deficiency is probably the most common deficiency in Australia but relatively little attention has been paid it: many multivitamin supplements don't even contain it. Deficiency is particularly significant for women, who are especially vulnerable if they eat poorly and have had a series of pregnancies without taking folate supplements. Often a diet deficient in folate will also be deficient in vitamin C, since the food sources tend to be the same.

FOOD SOURCES	Folate mcg*/100g
Bakers yeast	4000
Yeast extract	1000
Chicken liver	500
Lettuce	300
Lamb's liver	240
Spinach	140
Broccoli	110
Breakfast cereal	100
Almonds	96
Peas	78
Avocado	66

Notes
- Women who take oral contraceptives have lower-than-usual blood levels of folate. Evidence does not show, however, that these women have a deficiency or require folate supplements.

Function
- Involved in formation of red and white blood cells, production of gene-carrying material (DNA) in cells, and in growth promotion.

Deficiency
- Results in macrocytic anaemia, and damage to the lining of the small intestine, causing poor absorption.

Who is at risk?
- The institutionalised elderly, chronic alcoholics, and pregnant women (supplements appear desirable to maintain stores and provide for the increasing needs of the foetus).

Toxicity
- Large doses (in the order of 15 mcg/day) appear to be non-toxic, but may interfere with the diagnosis of pernicious anaemia.

RDI: 200 mcg total daily, with an additional 150–200 mcg during pregnancy and breastfeeding.

* mcg = micrograms

VITAMIN C

Vitamin C (ascorbic acid) is found in fresh fruits and some vegetables but is diminished by storage and cooking. Eat fruits fresh and vegetables raw or lightly cooked in a little water. The average Australian does not need extra vitamin C: two pieces of fruit and 4–5 serves of vegetables daily provides 3–8 times the RDI. However, there are people, especially elderly people who eat very little fruit and vegetables, for whom deficiency is a risk. The need for vitamin C is increased for smokers; they should include citrus fruits or juices in their diet.

Latest studies show that very large doses of vitamin C do not prevent colds but may reduce severity and duration slightly.

FOOD SOURCES	Vitamin C mg/100g
Guava	240
Capsicum	230
Blackcurrants	209
Broccoli	92
Brussels sprouts	83
Strawberries	58
Orange	53
Orange juice	47

Notes
- There is evidence that your body becomes dependent on large doses if you regularly take vitamin C supplements, and this can affect you adversely if you suddenly stop taking them. If you have been taking large doses for some time, tail them off gradually.

Function
- Promotes body connective tissue and normal development of bones and teeth.
- Role in manufacturing hormones and other compounds involved in transfer of nerve impulses.

Deficiency
- Scurvy – excessive bleeding, bruising, delayed wound healing, ulcers, drying of skin, susceptibility to infections, muscle weakness.

Who is at risk?
- Newborn infants, and young children on cow's milk.
- The institutionalised elderly, and tobacco smokers.

Toxicity
- Possible symptoms of toxic overdoses include kidney stones, vitamin B_{12} deficiency, blood clots, diarrhoea. Rebound scurvy may occur after stopping large doses.

RDI: 30–60 mg daily.

SAVING THE VITAMINS IN YOUR FOOD

Here are ways of handling food to maintain high vitamin content.

- Choose fruit and vegetables that are fresh and not overripe or bruised.
- Keep food in sealed containers in a cool, dark place.
- Don't peel or discard the outer layer of fruit and vegetables unless damaged or unpalatable.
- When cutting fruit and vegetables, keep the pieces as large as is practical.
- Cook with as little water as possible – it is not necessary to completely immerse the food.
- Cook for as short a time as possible and don't keep food hot for long periods of time.
- Don't cook at very high temperatures.
- Avoid the use of baking soda (bicarbonate of soda), which destroys vitamin C and nearly all the water-soluble vitamins.